LITERATURE FROM CRESCENT MOON PUBLISHING

Rethinking Powys: Critical Essays on John Cowper Powys
edited by Jeremy Mark Robinson

The Ecstasies of John Cowper Powys
by A.P. Seabright

Postmodern Powys: New Essays on John Cowper Powys
by Joe Boulter

Thomas Hardy and John Cowper Powys: Wessex Revisited
by Jeremy Mark Robinson

Sexing Hardy: Thomas Hardy and Feminism
by Margaret Elvy

Thomas Hardy's Jude the Obscure: A Critical Study
by Margaret Elvy

Thomas Hardy's Tess of the d'Urbervilles: A Critical Study
by Margaret Elvy

Thomas Hardy: The Tragic Novels
by Tom Spenser

Stepping Forward: Essays, Lectures and Interviews
by Wolfgang Iser

Lawrence Durrell: Between Love and Death, Between East and West
by Jeremy Mark Robinson

Andrea Dworkin
by Jeremy Mark Robinson

*German Romantic Poetry: Goethe, Novalis,
Heine, Hölderlin, Schlegel, Schiller*
by Carol Appleby

Cavafy: Anatomy of a Soul
by Matt Crispin

Rilke: Space, Essence and Angels in the Poetry of Rainer Maria Rilke
by B.D. Barnacle

Rimbaud: Arthur Rimbaud and the Magic of Poetry
by Jeremy Mark Robinson

Shakespeare: Love, Poetry and Magic in Shakespeare's Sonnets and Plays
by B.D. Barnacle

Feminism and Shakespeare
by B.D. Barnacle

The Poetry of Landscape in Thomas Hardy
by Jeremy Mark Robinson

D.H. Lawrence: Infinite Sensual Violence
by M.K. Pace

D.H. Lawrence: Symbolic Landscapes
by Jane Foster

The Passion of D.H. Lawrence
by Jeremy Mark Robinson

Samuel Beckett Goes Into the Silence
by Jeremy Mark Robinson

In the Dim Void: Samuel Beckett's Late Trilogy: Company, Ill Seen, Ill Said and Worstward Ho
by Gregory Johns

Andre Gide: Fiction and Fervour in the Novels
by Jeremy Mark Robinson

Julia Kristeva: Art, Love, Melancholy, Philosophy, Semiotics
by Kelly Ives

Luce Irigaray: Lips, Kissing, and the Politics of Sexual Difference
by Kelly Ives

Hélène Cixous I Love You: The Jouissance of Writing
by Kelly Ives

Emily Dickinson: *Selected Poems*
selected and introduced by Miriam Chalk

Petrarch, Dante and the Troubadours: The Religion of Love and Poetry
by Cassidy Hughes

Dante: *Selections From the Vita Nuova*
translated by Thomas Okey

Friedrich Hölderlin: *Selected Poems*
translated by Michael Hamburger

Rainer Maria Rilke: *Selected Poems*
translated by Michael Hamburger

AMOROUS LIFE

AMOROUS LIFE

John Cowper Powys
and the Manifestation of Affectivity

H.W. FAWKNER

CRESCENT MOON

Crescent Moon Publishing
P.O. Box 393
Maidstone
Kent
ME14 5XU, U.K.

First published 1998. Second edition 2008.
© H.W. Fawkner 1998, 2008.

The right of H.W. Fawkner to be identified as author of this book has been asserted generally in accordance with sections 77 and 78 of the Copyright, Designs and Patents Act 1988

Printed and bound in Great Britain
Set in Rotis Serif 9 on 13pt.
This book is part of the John Cowper Powys Studies Series.

All rights reserved. No part of this book may be reprinted or reproduced, stored in a retrieval system, or transmitted, in any form or by any means, electronic, mechanical, photocopying, recording or otherwise, without permission from the publisher.

British Library Cataloguing in Publication data

Fawkner, H.W. (Harald William), 1946-
Amorous Life: John Cowper Powys and the Manifestation of Affectivity. –
(John Cowper Powys Studies Series)
1. Powys, John Cowper, 1872-1963 – Criticism and interpretation
I. Title
828.9'12'09

ISBN 1-86171-1271
ISBN-13 1861711274

CONTENTS

1	*Owen Glendower*	11
2	*Weymouth Sands*	49
Bibliography		103

1

OWEN GLENDOWER

In *Owen Glendower* that which cannot be endured is at stake. Although the work terminates in the familiar Cowperist conception of enduring, the total impact is such that the idea of the possibility of enduring is shattered. The reiterated thematization of the idea of hating pain (912) has its origin not in some lack of pain-courage or pain-acquaintance but in knowledge of the depths of pain, of its Satanic bottomlessness. Broch's rejection of suffering – "I don't like *pain* ...I *don't* accept pain!" – originates in a visionary understanding of the inhumanity of pain. Pain's inhumanity is not really its capacity to create human suffering and to drag the human being down into a sub-human world of brutish negativity but rather the mystic god-quality triggering the felt notion that it perhaps has nothing to do with humanity whatsoever – that its horror is the horror of the extraneous. Pain is in this way an indwelling extraneousness in mankind, the dwelling-in-man of something so terrible that this terribleness necessitates a reassessment of life. The interesting thing about *Owen Glendower* is not only that writing now comes to be based on such a reappraisal, but that the terrible extraneousness of pain and evil now becomes part of the mythologization (in narrator as well as hero) which in former times had served the purpose of screening the beautiful soul from its ruination. So whereas the unthinkability of pain is present for Wolf as an *object* (the Waterloo face as an image), as an objectifiable unit of affectivity to be covered and concealed by supervening, more congenial units of affectivity, all replacing each other on the pleasure-continuum of the man of sensibility, the unthinkability of pain in *Owen Glendower* is held centrally in focus throughout the work as its affective ideativity.

The implications of the godlike pre-eminence of world-pain are metaphysical. A living organism in which the escalation of pain is infinite is an organism living its life "in a world where all is permitted"; and a world where all is permitted is metaphysically "a *universe* where all is allowed and nothing forbidden" (633; emphasis added). A *universe* is not simply a place, or even an infinitely big place. It is an order of things, a groundplan, an arrangement of life, a comprehensive life-patterning encompassing the laying-out of the crisscrossings of pleasure and pain, right and wrong, good and evil. The universe encountered by Wolf 'contains' evil, and disturbingly radical evil; but the world of *Owen Glendower* does not merely 'contain' pain, cruelty, and evil. It *is* this pain, cruelty, and evil through and through. This is not to say that there is no good, truth, or compassion. It is to say that truthfulness, joy, and tenderness make their appearance in the pain-universe in the way that the unlikely makes its appearance in the likely. When, after its release from unimaginable pain, the dog tortured by Gilles de Pirogue is given some water by Broch, goodness seems to spring unexpectedly from a foundation that in itself is untouched by goodness. The dog's releasement-expression is "the look of one who finds God at the bottom of Hell" (633). Here God is not the foundation. Hell is the foundation. And God, which for the dog is water, spills out of 'a crack' in a godless, indeed god-hating, universe.

> He – and he alone – had thought of *water*. Pouring this element from a metal flask into one of his great palms he knelt down and held it to the dog's mouth.
>
> *Lap! Lap! Lap!* There was no other sound for several minutes in that room. Twice, three times, four times, he filled his palm with water; while each time he did so the dog gave him a look that [Rhisiart] to the end of his days couldn't forget. It was more, not less than, a look of human gratitude. It was the look of one who finds God at the bottom of Hell. It was the look of one who finds a crack in a universe where all is allowed and nothing forbidden. And out of this crack water was coming. (633)

Although *Owen Glendower* is rich in historical detail and historical facticity, John Cowper is reluctant to historicize the universe (or multi-verse) as such. Hence there is perpetual irony in the narrator's deployment of theological dispute or social history as possible ground for ontological explication. The decline of chivalry, the destabilization of feudalism, and the installation of the anti-Pope cannot explain the *experience* of historical events any more than "the breaking down of faith" (624) can explain the merciless, soulless tortures monitored by 'scientists' like Gilles de Pirogue. It is as if these carefully-planned torments do not originate in the ones who invent and implement them but in an originary Hell-ground that is so deep that the very idea of finding a rational explanation is absurd. There *is* hellish cruelty *because* there is hellish cruelty. There *is* Hell because there *is* Hell. Hell causes itself. This causing-itself of Hell, examined intermittently throughout *Owen Glendower*, is foundational. There is no 'truth' about history which is not a foregrounding of this anomaly. Hence history is itself anomalous – and the first job of the historiographer is to come to terms with this anomaly, then to enter it, go right down to the bottom of it. Historiography can thus not remain what it normally is, a mere rationalization of the hellish (of war, blood, slaughter, persecution, organized malice, genocide). Nor can historiography be a celebration of Hell, an irresponsible grand tour of grotesque suffering and selfish machination. The anomaly is not there to be grasped or descriptively objectified. It is there to be recognized as auto-anomalized.

The auto-anomalizing of the anomaly called 'history,' the auto-anomalizing of civilization-time as pain and romance, is in the imagination a despotic craving for the moment of history as a moment of anomalized affectivity. The anomalizing of the moment – *Lap! Lap! Lap!* – is for a writer born in a civilization of Christian historiography an extrapolation of the pain of the crucifix (767). To take pain as life's originary anomaly is for such a historiographer to take pain as history's originary anomaly – an anomaly, in *Owen Glendower*, which turns the godhead away from himself – not into an abyss but into an anomaly. There is an aberration in life, in God. The aberration turns life toward the twisted lie that nourishes all creatures and all self-sensitized being. Yet matters are complex. "But when you take pain as the – as the basis of human life – and – and – as – as *the life of God* – there comes up – for it isn't *the whole of God* – something from underneath – that is – but what am I saying?" (768).

Various words and half-thoughts expressed more or less inadvertently in semi-significant theological dialogues have a tendency in *Owen Glendower* to leap out of their formal husks. They become darts freed from doctrine and dogma – and in this sudden unstereotyping of their dormant energy, they penetrate more than any philosophic 'news' from the mind of the narrator into the nerve-fabric of serious questioning. One such free-unit is the unit 'Marriage in Hell' (624); another is the free-unit 'new type of devil' (624). Is Gilles de Pirogue unleashed with the special design of heralding modernity, that phase in 'history' when pain will climb to a new summit of god-truth?

Femininity participates in the anomalizing. To call the moon "great Whore of Eternity" (645) is no longer to merely reactivate old stereotypes about the fickleness and instability of woman as truth. In *Owen Glendower* woman does not aspire to truth in the first place – or indeed to eternity and love. Here the paradigm of femininity is Lowri ferch Ffraid, illegitimate daughter of the prophetess of Dinas Bran – and once her character has become known, no one is surprised to learn that she co-authors the pain-science orchestrated by Gilles de Pirogue. To be a 'Whore' now is no longer to personify unfaithfulness, deviation from the norm. The norm itself is 'Whore' – and history is the whoreson living-out of the essence of this anomaly-as-norm. Lowri is not 'unfaithful.' She is not 'different' from history. Quite the contrary. She is the mother of history, the mother of anomaly. Her love, in other words cruelty-to-life, is the anomalizing of time and space that we call history. Technically speaking, Lowri is 'unfaithful' – untrue to husband, to lover, to morality, to justice, to Christian care. But ontologically speaking, seen in the historiographic context of the work's guiding metaphysics, Lowri is not 'unfaithful'; she is *faithful* to the anomaly that history *is*, that consequently the body too is, that consequently the *soul* is. It is the homecoming of the soul to the whoredom of creation's first nativity that pushes a shudder through *Owen Glendower* and through the *slow* reader who is willing to suffer. This does not mean that the work is strictly anti-Christian; it means, rather – and this is perhaps an ultimate extrapolation of the originary audacity of Christian ideativity – that there is 'somewhere' or 'not-somewhere' a counter-anomalous nativity parallel to the nativity of creation, that ultimate love (...*Lap! Lap! Lap!*...) is the other anomaly, an anomaly *so* anomalous that even the wickedness of creation cannot cancel it. This 'somewhere,' as 'not-somewhere,' is Wales. 'Wales' is a historiographic space that is withdrawn from the spacing of historiography. 'Wales' is a semi-supernatural *a priori* of geographic reality – Owen himself being the living spectre of this apriority, a ghost in history but also of history. He is the hero of the *anomalous* historiographer – of John

Cowper Powys as phantom-scribe recounting that which needs to be recorded on this side of the 'records' of history. This means that there is an escape from pain after all (...*Lap! Lap! Lap!...*), and that this escape is pre-inscribed in pain as its hidden underside.

However, this sense of an escape cannot rid itself of evil's tang. It is in the delineation of the imponderabilities attending the coping with evil that *Owen Glendower* reaches levels of felt reality that are nothing short of Shakespearean in their thrusting super-complexity. *Macbeth* is intermittently there in *Owen Glendower* as its nervous subtext. Because of his originary sidestepping of non-anomalous humanity, a king or a prince or a dwarf lives like pain itself on the level of the brute (...*Lap! Lap! Lap!...*) which has first-hand knowledge of everlasting evil (854). King Henry's Macbeth-like "*Who has done this?*" (854), spoken nightmarishly out of the pain of a Macbeth-like insomnia, is a despair that has beforehand materialized this side of psycho-physical horror – so that just as in *Macbeth* the aberration is felt to be cosmic-ontological and not merely personal. "*Who has done this?* Who has put *horns* upon Christ's head?" (854). Virtue itself is diabolical; hence those virtue-like features of life (such as sleep-time) that provide the soul with comfort, smoothness, and healing come to light not only as life-agony but as cosmic suffering. It is life itself that cannot sleep. King Henry's substantial soliloquy on sleep mirrors Macbeth's parallel disquisition. "What have they done then with poor Harry's sleep?" Glamis-Cawdor-King becomes Hereford-Lancaster-England. "Richard has it. Hotspur has it. The Duke, my father, has it ...But who will give it to Henry of Hereford, Brother? To Henry of Lancaster, Brother? To Henry of England, Brother?" (855). Powys seems to be following his West Country forerunner even in the detail of transubstantiating Macbeth's words on sleep as primary nourishment in life's feast: "Sleep's an easy thing to find. It's cheaper than ale. It's commoner than bread" (855). That which is stricken by the sleep-anomaly is not merely the king, a human being, a person, but existence as such: "Sleep's everywhere; isn't it, Brother? Isn't it, Grey Brother? Sleep's as wide as the air, as deep as the sea! What have they done then with poor Harry's sleep?" (855).

Importantly, monarchical insomnia is not reducible to the king's "devil" – "*Remorse*" (845). Had that been the case, insomnia as pain would have been thematically reducible to human pain. But it is precisely the point in this 'history' of Wales that pain is ultimately not 'caused' by anything whatsoever, except by pain itself. It is pain itself that causes pain. Hence pain is not to be thought of as something occurring 'in' the world or 'in' the universe. World and universe are at bottom nothing other than this auto-affectivity of pain affecting itself. This is why the narrator calls attention to the manner in which it is sub-human or semi-sub-human beings – and not Henry's peers – who 'respond' most vividly to the monarchical sleep-agony. "[B]oth the dwarf and the dog knew what the King was suffering. They had indeed been, so to speak, *inside his nerves* to a degree forbidden to any human creature" (854). Pain, even in these human-monarchial nerves, is not confined to the issue of tormented conscience. The pain belongs to Hereford and Lancaster, to air and space, to time and history. It quivers up through the paws of a small white greyhound; it shoots in mad zigzags through the spite and body-glee of a jesting dwarf (848); it throbs in morbid things like the bulb of "an evil plant" (846). If pain's evil makes an appearance in an Archbishop, its manifestation is not primarily an encirclement of his full Gestalt but a Dickensian objectification of itemizeable negativity – so that what asserts itself as evil is not the Archbishop but certain sinister "heavily-curved folds." These were "repeated *below* his eyes, and hung suspended there like fungus-growths beneath woodpecker holes" (846).

There is a Shakespearean heating-up of words to the alchemical level of hell-hot insanity. As the chanted linguistic units of the Weird Sisters are torn asunder by witchcraft into a frenzy of evil that atomizes not only the limbs and bodies but also the language that is thrown spitefully into the central cauldron, so in *Owen Glendower* the dwarf Hercule, like a "skipping red flea," enacts a pain-dance of black ecstasy that drives language itself to a hot condition of horrendous inexplicability.

> What [the dwarf Hercule] was pretending to do was to catch in his cupped fingers the prophetic words that issued from the mouth of the Friar and then to convey them in that same imaginary receptacle to the abstracted Archbishop, and having made as if he'd emptied them there like burning coals, to go skipping back to Mad Huw where he held out his hands as if to obtain another handful of these scoriac words.
>
> In this performance ...and apparently not to the King's displeasure, the butterfly-like dog took a lively part, leaping up at the dwarf. (853)

In the Worcestershire prison-cell, Mad Huw, feverishly mistaking King Henry for King Richard, has been holding up an idolized image of the latter to the former; but the result of this insult has not been the expected one, for the usurper, sinking abstractly back into the remorse of his murderousness, has joined up with Mad Huw in a reverie that blurs the line of distinction not only between King and usurper, between assassinated and assassin – but also between the good insanity of the mad Friar and the evil (but sleepless) sanity of the new king. "An appalling reciprocity rose up in that Worcestershire prison between Richard's murderer and Richard's idolater" (852). Throughout *Owen Glendower*, good and evil in this way reciprocate madly, playfully, and cruelly – as do sanity and insanity, pleasure and pain. In the prison-cell, the *evil* Archbishop, a man known for his merciless eagerness to put living freethinkers into tongs, hot flames and burning tar, cannot quite follow this collapsing of opposites. He is inferior to dog as well as to dwarf in the ability to grasp the becoming-mad of evil and the becoming-good of the infinitization of this self-sinking of evil into evil. Unlike the Archbishop, King Henry can reflect his own essential evil into an innermost evil-essence that is not itself evil ...but simply an essence, a felt, concrete, originary essentializing of all affectivity. This originary essence of affectivity is by no means exclusively human; nor does it really know good and evil as 'good' and 'evil.' "And mingled with this nervous confederacy in his [Henry's] own indictment, there was, as both dog and dwarf seemed perfectly to understand, a malicious satisfaction in the discomfort which the Friar's words must needs be causing the Archbishop" (852). The Archbishop understands the objectivity of the body, and this body-objectivity is in the world; it is organized as good-versus-evil, Christ versus anti-Christ, believer versus heretic, pleasure versus pain. But the Archbishop does not understand affectivity as such, that which is *on this side* of the world, refusing to enter it. He is thus left out in the cold – a mere political being, a mere creature-in-the-world, a mere manipulator of dialectical affects. Unlike the sleepless King, the mad Friar, the ecstatic dwarf, and the re-appearing ghost of the murdered monarch, the Archbishop does not have access to a pain *on this side* of the objective body, or to a pleasure-madness *on this side* of objective sensuality. The act of condemning the Lollard Walter Brut to death is thus an act that does not arise in King Henry as it arises in the Archbishop. For when Henry pronounces the verdict, Brut being unrepenting, he inadvertently touches that sensitized part of the soul which is not our sensitivity-in-the-world but our sensitivity-*on-this-side*-of-the-world, the sensitiveness which we share *absolutely* with animals because they too, in so far as they move in it, lack all merely-mundane reality. The dwarf becomes a symbol of this prehuman affectivity in which not only extreme pleasure but also extreme pain loosens us anomalously from human outline and from human contextualizations.

Certain bizarreries are overthematized to the point of becoming tedious. These include the 'fits' that come over the Prince and the 'blackness' that keeps paralysing his secretary. We learn that Rhisiart has decided to save Brut from the stake in one such moment of seeming unconsciousness – that the actual decision to empty the tiny phial of transparently tasteless poison into his friend's drink is taken when such a trance has been "on him" (857). But these reiterated references to the mind-absences fail to stir the alert reader into any mood of self-disturbance. In contrast, the more-Shakespearean, less psychologizing, moments of psychic oddness unsettle even the most hardened student of interior havoc. Such moments include the sight of the dwarf who notices the radical alteration of monarchical intonation when Henry's lips speak the word 'remorse' – the sight of this intently-watching dwarf as he breaks his attentiveness, leaps in three long hops to the king, crouches at his feet ...to set up a moan like the cry of a howling dog (850). Here the reader is left somewhat stranded, for there is no sure way in which to interpret the event; no real way of stabilizing the howling as something that might be confined to some certainizing category of psychological truth: empathy, sympathy, ironic hyperbole, etc. In the same way, the melodrama of Rhisiart's qualms about poisoning his Lollard companion is only going to stir the deeper feelings of a child-reader; but the "indescribable leer" of the executioner who is *not* presently going to be able to send Brut into unimaginable nuances of pain and pain-fright is a leer which, understood sharply at the level of the work's cruelty, is utterly disintegrating. It is the leer of "a good Christian writ backwards" (859). This writing-backwards of the good Christian, heralded in modern times by the rampages of Nietzsche, is no mere cult of the anti-Christ. Such an anti-cult would not be frightening, would not be a *leer*. The *leer* in *Owen Glendower*, the leering leer of a Lowri or a Gilles de Pirogue, betokens no antithesis, no negation, no rejection of this or that. The writing-backwards of Christianity is not a negation of Christianity ...for in this backward-writing what is written, letter by letter, is still Christianity, is still, in a sense, *good* Christianity. We may thus entertain the justified suspicion that, all being said and done, the human being who prides himself on being able at short notice to help individuals like Master Brut into flames and people like Rhisiart into rope is nothing less than a fully-Christian being, a rather likeable fellow, one who ultimately has no more (and no less) blood on his hands than the Prince of Wales, than the archetypal scribe himself, Oxford-bred Rhisiart ab Owen.

"[A]ccept a good Christian's congratulation! Of course, as a professional man

– which is, as you might say a good Christian writ backwards" – and the fellow gave Rhisiart an indescribable leer that was at once sympathetic and avaricious – "a man might complain ...at having to rise with the cock to take down an unblooded scaffold and as pretty a pile of dry withies as this town has ever seen. But, as I've always said, 'tis the hand that signs the warrant, not the hand that piles the faggots, that keeps the smell of the burning in his beard." (859).

Rhisiart too is writ backwards here; for his release from the gallows has been made possible by an act of infidelity on the part of Tegolin. This infidelity, no less than the 'blackness' in which the hero has chosen to accept it, is a *leer* – a smearing-out of the difference between truth and untruth, between Christian suffering and Christian suffering writ backwards. This backward-writing of Christian suffering – is it a suffering? In what direction does it point us? Such questions are the asking-matter of *Owen Glendower*; but they are also the matter of the asking that makes such a work possible in the first place. *Owen Glendower* is not simply a historiography 'in which' certain ontological, theology-oriented questions are reviewed. The work is rather itself prompted by a *re*-viewing of the world and of that which makes it possible, *viz.*, affectivity.

•

In *Owen Glendower*, the following assertion is paradigmatic: "Life, with such as he abroad, has no defence, no justification" (671). Since "he," Gilles de Pirogue, is the kind of being who is abroad, life simply has no defence. But a life that has no defence, our life, nevertheless has to be *lived*. We live and are alive in a life that has no defence; we move freely in a region of deeds which is a region lacking justification; but this region lacking justification is still a region: it has its hills, its mountains, its moments of love (all of them potentially cruel), its homes, castles, fortresses, firesides, utensils, medicines, gardens, rivers, moons, stars, horizons. In life's lack of self-justification, the self, itself lacking all defence, is "abroad" (671). "Life, with such as he *abroad*, has no defence, no justification". The terribleness of the being-abroad of selfhood is by no means confined to those who, like Gilles de Pirogue, uphold "a doctrine of devils" (671). It is the being-abroad of the self itself that is the founding terror – and for some reason the contemplative life, in *Owen Glendower*, is no protection from this terrible being-abroad. Since the contemplative mind (Glyn Dwr himself) is drawn out into history and world, there is no history-free place for contemplation to withdraw to. In *Owen Glendower* there is an *a priori* mundanizing of the contemplative life – so that this life, in temperate Friar as well as in tranced Prince, is drawn and extended into the spatializing temporality of history, world, and world-history.

The being-abroad of life as a being-abroad of life's lack of justification is in this work the being-abroad of the human eye. There is a sustained preoccupation with human eyes. Pairs of eyes negotiate a sense of the equivocation of a gaze. The gaze points to the 'light' of the self as a light lacking defence. The 'light' of the human eye lacks defence. It is with the 'light' of such an eye that Gilles de Pirogue gazes at the helpless torture-victims of his experiments – experiments which are nothing other than scenarios created *for* such an eye and *for* such an eye's light. It is with the 'light' of such an eye that there is eye-to-eye contact in the sick 'passions' between Lowri and her ...what shall we call them? ...victims. Whereas in the animal there is no tacit reciprocation of the 'light' of this eye-without-justification, in the human being there is. This applies to Lowri's 'lovers' – but also to those seemingly neutral individuals who appear to be mere disinterested or at least contingent spectators. Thus when we are told that Rhisiart "stared" into the "wolfish" eyes of the *Sin-Eater* (671), the reader has travelled far enough into the terrible 'light' of the work itself to sense that the hero by no means remains uncontaminated by the terribleness of this light. In *Owen Glendower*, staring, in the sense of witnessing, is by no means a mere observing. This fact extends all the way to the reader – one who, much like "our friend" (Rhisiart), is inadvertently on friendly terms with horror. "Our friend" Rhisiart is in this way "our friend" life – that which lacks justification. There is no defence of life – and the narrator eventually drives home the point that in his ugliest moment of weakness, "our friend" has no defence. This "friend" who is "our" friend only makes an appearance by means of the 'light' of the eye of a reader – one who *gazes*, gloats. This gazing of life's gaze into life's gaze is in *Owen Glendower* driven to a vertigo known nowhere else in the writings of John Cowper. The contemplative mind grows dizzy in this inward-whirling of life, losing all contemplative essence. It is of the essence of contemplation that it is not giddy. The contemplative eye is essentially not a giddy eye – but a tranquil gaze which, if it cannot immobilize the world, at least can immobilize its own æsthetization of the world. This æstheticizing of the world, or originary beholding of the world's self-æstheticizing, is debarred from the reading, narrating, and fictional activity of *Owen Glendower*. The work's contemplative-readerly perspective is sucked into the cruel subject matter of its raw historical materiality – not through some clever trick of metafiction or narratological contriving, but through the gaze itself, its collapsibility, its 'light.'

Because of the luminous collapsibility of the gaze, there is in *Owen Glendower* a visionary refusing-to-see in seeing itself. This event is not a screening of seeing from sights that are too horrible for the eye to behold. It is not a partial blinding of the eye itself but a recognition of a "lidlessness" ("lidless eyes," 719) in the moment of visualization. In this lidlessness, as in the semi-opaque stare of a fish, there is a primordially submerged equalizing of open staring and absolutely blind unseeing – as if seeing, now, is no longer an act but itself a condition of pain, a primary numbness that looks through the spontaneity of its own dullness with the acute intelligence of a beastly but also divine eye-suffering. Such lidlessness, originary opening of sight as unprotected non-sensitivity of first sensing, is rendered in a memorable sequel to news informing us that the French Chancellor has dispatched "a marvellous great ape" to Owen (719). In the hands of Gilles de Pirogue, this "Marvel of Creation" has suffered "pains unspeakable." As the Prince of Wales stares at the sea from the narrow window of his chamber, he thinks of the letter announcing the arrival from Brittany of this ape. As he does so, the narrator expands the work's thematization of the motif of pain by permitting the Prince's mind to return to a sight seen on the previous day: the dead body of a stranded porpoise, devoured on the beach by seagulls. In his moment of imaginary commentary, Owen visualizes birds of the air as creatures capable of collapsing the difference between sea-creatures and land-creatures (719). Air and death conjointly wipe out the difference between water and earth. But where does *suffering* situate itself in this map of air-earth-water-death? For "some reason" the Prince of Wales visualizes an abortive rescue-operation, in which the "marvellous great ape" from Brittany falls into the sea after being saved from its torturer. But the sea-creatures refuse to eat it. Why is this so? Why do the creatures of the sea refuse to devour "a creature like an ape" as it struggles for life in the water? The idea of this struggle against drowning *rather* than against being devoured sticks in the Prince's mind "with a curious pain. Amid gills and fins and lidless eyes in jelly-like slime, and undulant slipperinesses gliding through ooze and silt, how painful to think of the struggles of a warm-blooded hairy ape!" (719). We find out nothing about the eyes of the "marvellous" ape. But we find out something about the eyes of those creatures who, without interfering, witness the exquisite panic of its watery descent. These onlooking eyes are "lidless." There seems to be no pain in these lidless eyes, the missing lid being perhaps the absence of the self-sensitizing difference between the open and the closed, sensitivity and indifference, pain and numbness, affectivity and life *lower than* affectivity. Perhaps, rather, there is a submersion of affectivity in itself – a submersion that is so oceanic, so abyssal, so 'wet,' that we can only picture it in a moment of horror that is itself slimelike, 'hairy,' undulant, and lidless. No sea-creature, no land-creature like Gilles de Pirogue, needs to inflict any devouring pain on the "warm-blooded hairy ape." Its struggle *for* life is like the struggle *of* life: pain struggling with pain, affectivity affecting affectivity. The "struggles of a warm-blooded hairy ape" occur *on this side* of history. They are not struggles in any ordinary, mundane sense. They are the lidlessness of auto-affection, pain sinking with and without struggle into itself. This, and nothing else, is the main concern of *Owen Glendower*.

●

Perhaps lidlessness is related in some way to Owen's status as "wizard" of "the forces of destruction in the unseen world" (673). His "devilish power over water and fire and wind" may be a mere myth, spread by "rumours" (673); but these rumours are somehow interior to his life, to his political credibility. It is important that Owen be a function of black magic, 'blackness' not being in fact reducible to the idea of being "possessed of supernatural powers" (673). Owen's political 'blackness' is part and parcel of the overall thematization of the idea of affirmative imposture. Owen is certainly an impostor – and his political manipulation of Tegolin as Maid in Armour shows how far he is ready to go in the direction of mythological deception. Yet, as we have already seen, the counterfeit is in *Owen Glendower* an act of truth – as it is in the deeds of the artist. Not only æsthetics and historiography – John Cowper as counterfeit historiographer of 'Wales' – but also theology and ontology are drawn into the question of imposture. If imposture is in a queer way originary – even in love, even in the life of God as the life of affectivity – then deeds of fraud such as that performed by Father Rheinalt for Catherine's dying Nurse are not humbug. In the monk's inadvertent imitation of Saint Peter, prompted by the fraudulent words spoken to the expiring woman by Broch – "the Saint has come himself!" (579) – there is an ontology of imposture deep enough to be taken as foundational. This ontology of imposture requires a flexing of the rigidity of reason – a species of tolerance that makes way for a shielding of the spirit from a worse imposture – from reason itself. The moment of religious vision is now not so much an instant of revelation, heralded by trumpets, comets, and cosmic quakings – but a goofy freak-moment. The gawky showing reveals the divine by means of the missing dissimulation *of* dissimulation. There is no dissimulation in 'Saint Peter' – for 'Saint Peter' takes no precautions whatsoever to enhance the counterfeit reality that 'he' (Father Rheinalt) *happens* to be. Father Rheinalt happens to be Saint Peter in the way that Owen *happens* to be Prince of wizards and devilish powers ...in the way that Tegolin *happens*, without much far-fetched faking, to be Maid in Armour. 'History,' now, is simply the perfectly contingent moment. 'History' is the moment of perfection in which circumstances collaborate to produce an effect that gives chance and semblance the outline of destiny and and truth. Returning from fishing, Father Rheinalt rises out of pond-reeds with mud and duck-weed smeared all over his naked thighs, with a great fishing pole in his hand, and half-a-dozen fine striped perch strung around his neck (577). Ushered by Broch into the dying Nurse, who has been crying for a priest, Father Rheinalt instantaneously prompts the deathward soul to utter the words of confession in order to be definitively absolved from sin.

> Rhisiart was close behind him now and when he heard the familiar words – 'In the name of the Father and of the Son and of the Holy Ghost' – issuing from the lips of that passionate and simple man, with five mud-smelling fish hung round his neck and his legs slimy with pond-weed, he was more religiously stirred than he'd been since that Midsummer Day when he heard Mass with Tegolin and Mad Huw.
> And in a way he couldn't explain, and never was able to explain, the authoritative apparition of this invoker of "*Pater-Filius-Spiritus*," bursting out through the slime of a fish-pond and surrounded by the blood-stained gills of five perch – 'all of them,' as the good man was certain to boast ere long, 'weighing nearly a pound' – added a new and paradoxical force to the irritable and inconsequential reactions roused in him by the convincing arguments of Master Brut. (579-580)

Brut is a rationalist believer. His faith is based on principles of no-nonsense argumentation. In an important sense, however, the life of God and the life of history are in *Owen Glendower* based on nonsense. The rampant nonsensicality of battle, jealousy, love, and redemption are not of the order of the reason-oriented insanities perpetrated on sentient beings by the likes of Gilles de

Pirogue and his 'scientific' peers. There is no imposture at all in these rationalist experiments. They may take place away from the public eye; but they are absolutely uncounterfeited *vis-à-vis* themselves. By contrast, 'Saint Peter' is *pure* counterfeit – an anomaly of mind, matter, and adoration.

In the death-moment, monitored spiritually by the counterfeit 'Saint Peter,' the Nurse's face immobilizes itself as a face "imprinted with the certainty of redemption" (580). Understood in this way, "the Christian mystery" (693) is an outcome of reduction. The mystery has *reduced* itself – through inadvertently goofy imposture – to something that is 'refined,' but 'refined' now not in the sense of appearing sophisticated but in the sense of appearing cut down to the quick of its barest essence. There is an awkwardness, almost a crudeness in this reductive cutting-back of mystery. The Prince of Wales is himself crossed by this intersecting of 'refinement' as cutting-fine (appearing even in the fastidious caressing of the forked beard) and 'refinement' as gross reduction. As mood, this latter event is one which "his subtlest introspection could scarcely follow" (693). The gross form of 'refinement' expresses itself as a motion toward the 'blackness' of non-being, as a move "to reduce himself to non-existence" (694). In one such mood, "Owen had rejected all armour, all weapons, and had attired himself completely in black" (694).

Although he now appears like "a demon-worshipping student of alchemy in some lonely tower in the Hartz mountains," and although his self-reduction is at once expressive of a "longing" for political success *and* a "passion" for Tegolin (694), the work does not really encourage us to entertain some naivistic, twentieth-century view of such holding-back as a holding-back of sexuality. For the driving force in Owen, indeed in life, is not sexual energy but reduction itself. Reduction itself is 'sexual' ...in the same way that it itself is 'historical,' 'religious.' Reduction is not expressive of some sexual aberration. Quite the contrary, the sexually bizarre situation is expressive of reduction. Reduction is in this way a clue to life as such and in general. It may express itself in different, indeed opposite, ways – the painwardness of Owen, the deathwardness of Broch; but it is itself primary, not a 'symptom.'

Such remarks are pertinent for interpreting the strangely complex affectivity-aureole that encircles Owen's daughter Catherine before, during, and after her renunciation of love (of Rhisiart). The reduction of Catherine is an event in which she puts her unloved future husband, and indeed the entire remainder of her existence, "*between herself and her life*" (590). This reduction is paradigmatic in *Owen Glendower*. Catherine's life is cut back by politics. The cutting-back expresses itself as running. As affectivity, Catherine finds herself running from affectivity. In the Forests of Tywyn, affectivity runs from affectivity. This running-from-affectivity is Catherine (590). But this running-from-affectivity is also affectivity. There is in affectivity *itself* (in Catherine as love) an escape from affectivity. This is, in a manner of speaking, a 'blackening' of affectivity – its sinking into a medium of self-vanishing which by the same token is the immanence of a new manifestation ...a new *black* manifestation: black, humid, auto-affective. "But the wet grasses dragged at her feet, and the soaked mosses like great undulating sea-sponges dragged at her ankles, and the gaping tree-roots full of jet-black watery mouths sucked at her knees, and the tall trees waved mesmeric arms towards her thighs" (590). On account of the vanishing of the world, of the prospect of mundane happiness, affectivity now has no 'place.' Landscape has been sucked into its own dark centre. There is a queer immobilization of life and of emotion. In this immobilizing, the future comes to a halt. The halting of time, the pure vanishing of expectancy, indeed of history – is not a suspension. There is no hesitation. As moment, 'blackness' is not a rupture in time, some sort of limit. Instead there is simply a curving-in of time and history as affectivity – a withholding promising ...blackness. The blackness is not a darkness. It is not a form of obscurity. It is the fullness of affectivity as such – an affectivity soaking itself in the dusk of its own pure perspirations. Here the "whitish drops" of the mist are not units of whiteness but of affectivity, of dusk, in fact of 'blackness.' They arise in a forest without 'light' – being light-without-light. The "dusky shell-like curves" of woman are not so much the forms of femininity as the in-curving shape of a self-immobilized dusk-affectivity. Catherine sinks down beneath an immense oak that is absolutely immobile. "Scarce any foliage had this tree lost, but from all its twigs and from many of its leaves the mist hung in whitish drops, drops that were forever quivering in their fall but which never fell. Her lover breathed long and deep, gazing down at the vaporous blur that was her face and at the dusky shell-like curves that made up her unresisting form" (591).

Only if Catherine's father is allied with the Mortimers, will there be a liberation of Wales (583). Accordingly, Catherine is a prisoner of the paternal politics of Owen. She is obliged to marry Sir Edmund Mortimer. But the one who inadvertently imprisons her heart, Sir Edmund, is himself a prisoner of war (576). Sir Edmund is a "black figure" (577, 599). The prison-feeling expresses an overall sense of self-imprisonment in the work, in 'history,' in 'Wales,' ...indeed in love, in affectivity itself.

"Sir Edmund ...was standing on the balcony in front of his window ...You must remember the man's still a prisoner of war. I've never seen him leave the house unattended ...He stands for half the day on that balcony. It's roofed-over, but it faces the rain ...I think he'd be *glad* if he caught his death by exposing himself on that balcony! I don't like seeing his black figure forever standing there, nor does Father Rheinalt. And you can see it from such a long way off! Down the pine-avenue you can see it. Down the linden-avenue you can see it. And you can see it from Merlin's elm." (576-577)

Sir Edmund's "black figure" (577, 599) is contextualized within a constellation of black units: the "black tonsured head" of Father Rheinalt (577), the "darkness within darkness" of the Rector of Byford mounted on his horse (600), the "tenebris" and "umbra mortis" of ecclesiastical forest-chanting (600) ...and the "expectant black slugs" of autumn itself (600). Here in the Forests of Tywyn, the 'blackness' of the feeling of autumn has come to sink so deeply into *itself* – that there is virtually nothing other left to feel than an all-encompassing sinking-into-itself of autumn in autumn, of forest in forest, of feeling in feeling, of blackness in blackness. 'Blackness' is colour but also obliteration, compressing-into-self in self, in compression, in 'blackness.' There is in *Owen Glendower* a 'blackening' that is not merely a darkening, absencing, or deadening but a collapsing, without inwardness, of world into ...something. The name of this something is 'Wales,' 'Tywyn,' 'Owen.' Because this blackness-collapse is no strict inwardness, it can remain a display – it can show itself, become manifest, *appear*. The Forests of Tywyn certainly *appear*. 'Wales' certainly *appears*. Owen himself certainly *appears*. The sense of 'balcony' is the ideal platform for this open displaying-of-itself of that which sinks away from the world. Hence the "black slugs" too have "their balconies" (600). 'Balcony' is the elevation of sinking-in to the altitude of a dignified showing of an affectivity lacking all light, all luminosity, all 'height.'

> '*Inluminare his qui in tenebris et in umbra mortis sedent*' ...here he [Rhisiart] was listening while the phantom echoes of ecclesiastical unction sank out of hearing.
> It seemed to him as if in that dense darkness the ghosts of those resonant Latin syllables were uttering querulous moans and plaintive whimperings as they settled down among the expectant black slugs, waiting for them *on their balconies* on the under-side of the fallen leaves!

And he was aware, too, of a persistent and mortuary smell of funguses ...Autumn lasted longer in the Forests of Tywyn than anywhere else in the world ...And since the extent of the Forests of Tywyn was so vast, the mass of vegetation with its sweet, sickly, autumnal smell, never *quite* obliterated by the other seasons, was correspondingly vast; and so now on this particular day, when the wild winds sank down and the persistent rains ceased, the whole forest became one all-dissolving, all-absorbing, all-unfathomable *fungus*. (600-601)

Here the words "never quite obliterated" suggest that *obliteration* (biological decomposition) was never *quite* obliterated. Obliteration as auto-affectivity is the inability of obliteration (of autumn) to obliterate itself (to vanish). Instead obliteration deepens, continues, sinks farther into itself. In this general sinking-as-obliteration and in this general obliteration-as-sinking, the sense that "the wild winds sank down" does not really suggest a cessation-feeling. For although the sinking of wild winds is technically speaking a cessation of their full force and unimpeded wildness, this sinking in the wind is on the level of the work's affectivity precisely a missing cessation – an actual continuation *of sinking*, a celebration of the auto-affectivity of sinking as *sinking*, of the 'eternity' of sinking. The sense of cessation in the line telling us that "the wild winds sank down and the persistent rains ceased" is *immediately* cancelled by the much larger sense of the sinking-depth of the hush into which autumn now submerges itself ...totally, unconditionally.

The pages that follow are among the finest in John Cowper's fiction. Catherine is to be married to Sir Edmund Mortimer, a prisoner of war. He is a personification of sadness – of the sadness of history. As lovers torn away from each other by the necessities of politics, Catherine and Rhisiart are themselves drawn into sadness. "[All] the days of that November were pitiable and shameful days for Rhisiart and indescribably tragic days for Catherine" (601). Yet by aiming its regard at the stoic, elevated, and distant figure of Mortimer, the sadness of politically ruined love swiftly finds itself drawn into a 'blackness' that does not really emanate from its own pain but, strangely, ideatively, from blackness as object and silhouette. Rhisiart is "astonished" to find that Catherine, without being attracted to Mortimer, is frequently to be seen in his company. Her entire being – a being that is now 'black' – has been shifted over into sadness ...sadness not as self-pity but as distance. The "black figure of the man on the balcony" (590) is no longer alone on the sadness-horizon. "She would be always at his side, with her ungloved hand on

Mortimer's black sleeve, standing in the covered porch watching the rain, or seated together in some black oaken chair in the library with some great illuminated folio on their knees, but both pairs of eyes fixed upon vacancy" (602). The affectivity of distance is now the felt emotion sadness, the black. Conversely the affectivity of black sadness is now the felt farawayness of distance. However, since distance is as black as sadness, it becomes unworldly – lacking extension. In the collapse of distance into distance-without-extension, distance becomes something 'near.' Like the "great" folio, sadness is "illuminated" by the 'intimacy' (nearness without rapprochement) of distance. Without the stir of any volition, desire, or even sadness-feeling, Catherine and Mortimer come to negotiate a domain of feeling which, despite being devoid of all passion, is pure affective life.

> Nobody ever saw them talk to each other. Catherine's eyes would follow Rhisiart everywhere, and would search for him if he wasn't there; while Mortimer's eyes would be fixed on any object: a window, a door, a fragment of tapestry, a picture, through which he could stare into some receding horizon.
> Mortimer's courtesy towards her was exquisite. Rhisiart saw him do little things for her that he himself had never done. And though they never conversed, they often exchanged a word, or a look, or even a smile. (602)

Mortimer's courtly melancholia is quintessentially the affectivity of farawayness. When the Princess of Wales weds him, she enters into communion with distance itself. The marriage bed is a site where this distance becomes *phenomenon*. But this phenomenon, in phenomenalizing itself, is not itself extended in space ...as distance is. It is instead the pointlike, unextended sound of prayer. This sound is not emitted by the language of prayer, by its phonic nimbus, but by something closer to the affectivity of prayer as such. Here, "in almost complete darkness," phenomenalization has vanished by means of melancholia's reduction of itself to its own *heard* (but still unphonic) vanishing-point. The *click-click* is not a voice. Nor is it countable ...being itself, in the featherweight instant of its pure moment (*click-click*), no more singular than plural, no more plural than singular.

> A gentleman of the old tradition was Sir Edmund; and he was already moving to the small oratory concealed by heavy curtains, whither his personal possessions had been conveyed! Here, in almost complete darkness,

he remained so long on his knees that a far less gallant girl than Catherine would have had all the respite she required.

As she lay in Rhys Ddu's great ancestral bed, her sea-green eyes wide open and staring at the steady candle-flames reflected in a shield above the smouldering hearth, she could hear the *click-click* of Mortimer's rosary as he told his beads. (611)

The visual, equally non-sonorous, counterparts of the clicks are "the tiny points of redness" of the candles that have just been extinguished in the bridal chamber (612). Like the click, the redness is a phenomenalization of the reduction of phenomenological distance to a minimalistic one-pointedness. In this one-pointedness, melancholia is divested of extension – so that the bride and the bridegroom find themselves released into a pure, 'non-emotive' intimacy. Catherine and Mortimer do not 'feel' anything for each other; but precisely for this reason they come to know the pure affective life, life as affective absolute only. This absolute life is concrete, and it phenomenalizes itself here as *slight* movement. "Catherine slid a little nearer"; Mortimer "now sat up in the bed, arranging his pillow behind his back and crossing his legs" (613). The "inevitableness of a movement" is intimacy's auto-affection (613). The inevitable here is not that which destiny has grandly and impersonally decided, but pre-reflective body-motion *per se*. As Mortimer begins to play Provençal tunes on his lute, there is a phenomenalization of movements preserving an all-important lack of significance in them. The hand "holding" the lute, the body that Catherine "slid" a little nearer, the hand that he "slipped" round her, the flickerings that "crossed" his face – these phenomena do not arise in 'the world' but in pure movement, movement reduced to the rudimentary "embers" of its truth (615). The lute does not introduce any forceful sense of sonorous reverberation into this scenario. The words 'lute,' and 'Provençal' foreground a courtly sense of melodic extenuation, a sense of an extenuation *of* the melodic, a sense of archaic stylization – the mediæval adumbration of something too delicate and distilled to be called music, to be simply 'heard.' There is an inhering sadness in 'lute,' a sadness that lies alongside the married couple, shielding them. Hence the play of movements in bride and bridegroom is not valorized as a carnal fusion of bodies existing in 'the world' but as a passing of the outline of melancholia as distance into an outline of a melancholia lacking distance. This distanceless melancholia – "tiny points of redness" (612) – is an unglazed immanence devoid of presence ...but also, because of compressive 'blackening' and immobilization, devoid of absence. The transcendent 'out there' of the theatre of sadness ('history,' fate, predestination, deathwardness) has no longer any stage or balcony for the purpose of its exhibition of itself to self or world. 'Balcony' has stepped this side of the world ...and is now 'alcove.'

> The young man lay on his back staring at the unglazed window from which an air that seemed almost frosty was blowing in; and the young girl lay on *her* back staring at the tiny points of redness and the wisps of blue smoke of the extinguished candles, and at the fire-light shadows flickering about the walls ..."only you must let me do everything I want to first!" ...But this "everything" he wanted ...had to do, it seemed, with re-lighting the candles, visiting the alcove where he had left his belongings and getting into bed again with a Provençal lute in his hand. He now sat up in the bed, arranging his pillow behind his back and crossing his legs; and in this position, while the candle-flames were again reflected in the crusader's shield, he began playing on the lute. (612-613)

•

I have intermittently been calling attention to the 'unphonic.' A *phonon* is a quantum of vibrational energy in crystals. It is not sonant, not sonorous. When *Owen Glendower* sports various reverberations that lack sonorousness, such unacoustic micro-events do not fall into the work like random meteorites whose trajectories happen to cross the orbit of the writer's imagination. Instead the unacoustic reverberation is emitted from the work's core. It has something to say about the distinctiveness of the work's personality and about the genius of its composite strangeness. When Prince Henry enters the inner room of the Rose and Crown after the unexpected retreat of Glendower's army from the outskirts of Worcester, Madge Howlet and Bess Bolt, the two whores of the Rose and Crown, discuss the queer twitching of the thin, monarchical lips. "Madge maintained that when he spoke it was like a moor-fowl crossing a stream: 'The ripples go on spreading after the bird's flown!' Bess had a less homely comparison. She said it was like *seeing an echo*. 'His lips,' she assured them, 'echo every word he utters, only without a sound!'" (839). When John Cowper Powys italicizes a cluster of words in this manner, it is convenient to imagine that such an event is little more than the whim of a creative mind given to a variety of eccentric impulses – each one just about as neurotic as the monarchical tick. But the italicizing of "*seeing an echo*" is in point of fact no chance event. It is in the moments of seemingly unmotivated emphasis that we find clues to the artifact. To *see an echo* is to behold an acoustic image lacking acoustic phenomenalization, to ideatively witness unsonorousness as 'empty' reverberation. There is a sighting of the acoustic absence; and this sighting, as a revelation of the *empty* essence of reverberation, is phenomenon. The withdrawing of acoustic plenitude seems to have to do with a general withdrawal of sonorousness from language – with a general withholding of *language* from language. Moreover, this emptying-out of language, *its reduction to affective seeing*, is in a strange and somewhat disturbing manner related to sexuality, indeed to promiscuous, indiscriminate, unrestrained sexuality. "[H]e paused while his lips moved in that same silent twitching that Madge and Bess had noticed even while he was making free with them" (840). Making-free with loose women, *monarchical* making-free with loose women, is somehow an unacoustic making-free ...a making-free in which the loosening of language from acoustics and the loosening of sexuality from order are one and the same loosening, one and the same reverberatory *emptying*.

It is unlikely that such matters are reducible to sex, to the work's thematization of the "human aberrations" of gloating, sadomasochist sex-thrills and other forms of "perilous perversity" (903). Thus, in the scene depicting the circumstances of the humiliating sexual submission of Tegolin to Master Shore (a man whose influence in court will facilitate a pardon for her sentenced husband), the image of stairs sprinkled with candle-grease is not reducible to the dark sex-feeling of this sinister scenario. In Powys, as in Dickens, an individual *thing* can emerge all on its own into a thingly pre-eminence defying all contexts – particularly contexts that are phonic, linguistic, vocal. The image of "Tegolin, with her red braid pressed between her white shoulders and a strange bed, submitting to the final outrage" is quite conventional, even predictable. So are the young woman's feelings, "what she felt when she climbed those stairs to the armourer's open door" (837). But the image of *the sprinkled candle-grease itself* is by no means conventional, or indeed predictable.

> Tegolin was a warm-blooded girl, and she never had been a girl of morbidly virginal shrinkings. But save for her romantic idealizing of the Friar she had given herself to Rhisiart, body, soul, and spirit, to such an absolute *tune* that it would have been hard to make another woman – even Lady Mortimer – understand what she felt when she climbed those stairs to the armourer's open door.

> The worthy man had rallied her the next morning about the candle-grease with which the stairs were sprinkled; but she didn't confess to him how many times she had descended, before the final blind rush that took her to the top. (837; emphasis added)

In the hesitant descending-and-ascending, ascending-and-descending, there is an element of fascination that is not reducible to sexuality, to trepidation, or indeed to any other feeling. Although the sprinkled candle-grease obviously reverberates within human emotion, being a sign pointing to guilt, fear, nausea, and other forms of affect, it also reverberates in an *absolute* dimension, which, like the "absolute tune" of love itself, is not the human-acoustic sphere of voices, sounds, and sonorities but the unhearing absoluteness of affectivity as such. Rhisiart is saved from the barrels of tar and the red-hot prongs – themselves absolute, hallucinatory, unacoustic – by a woman who has performed "the sacrifice of honour to life" (837); but what is given to Rhisiart is in fact something more absolute than life. For whereas 'life' is something weaker than the barrels of tar and the red-hot prongs, the affectivity of the stairs sprinkled with candle-grease is not. In giving herself to the influential armourer, Tegolin becomes part of a a pure affective commotion that madly overreaches any 'feelings' that she could possibly have had about 'honour,' 'life,' 'death,' or 'love.' This very madness is embedded in the image of the stairs sprinkled with candle-grease. This grease *remains*. And it remains precisely as *grease*.

Something similar may be said about the straw mentioned a moment earlier. Here Tegolin is crouching above the weary form of her imprisoned husband, one knee on the flag-stones, the other on the straw of his bed (835). When she slowly rises, lifting one knee from the stones and the other from the straw, something flits "across" Rhisiart's consciousness: "Do nuns have straw to kneel on, like cows in a shed?" (836). The image has a Shakespearean quality – so that we sense that *on this side* of our reflective powers *this very act of visualization* is burning reason away. Tegolin's sensualism now has to be measured, recognized, and indeed perceived, across the suggestive alterity of this surreal straw-conceit. We read the following innocent-looking lines *after* having encountered 'straw.'

> But she rose to her full height now, lifting her hands to her head to coil up her braid. To do this she removed another bodkin, and, because her fingers were busy, held it in her mouth till its time had come, staring at Rhisiart

from above the tightened lips out of which it protruded. She had thrown her mantle aside when she first entered, and her pale blue gown, caught up below her breasts by a gold band, displayed to their best advantage her soft white throat and rounded arms, and even those tiny freckles on her skin of which Glyn Dwr had made so much. (836)

There is nothing unbalanced or asymmetric about this passage; indeed, it displays the assured descriptive powers of Powys's measured, straight-forward prose. But because the paragraph is released into phenomenalization by the strange question, "Do nuns have straw to kneel on, like cows in a shed?", the reader has to view the manifestation of Tegolin's sensual presence from a 'prostration' of reading in which reading itself is absurdly kneeling – but kneeling to do *what*? The beholding of Tegolin becomes more than a readerly beholding. It is beforehand fraught with a touch of abandon and a sense of innocent-illicit mischief that is no less surreal than the image of nuns kneeling in straw. Subjectivity, that which kneels in straw, that which in reading or loving is initiated into an imaginative receptivity which does not screen such ideas, is a lower-order instantiation of the figure-on-the-balcony affectivity encountered earlier in the Forests of Tywyn (590). To be a nun kneeling on straw, to be a sad prison-figure on a balcony: these modes of being phenomenalize themselves in acts that are, as it were, the upper and lower tier of a selfsame strangeness – humanity seen in hermeneutic regions of emotionally unexplored incarceration, souls seen as entities marooned in themselves as strangeness and as pure idea ('nun,' 'prisoner of war,' 'wife'). Perhaps this is what existence is – as soon as 'history' is conceived as a free locking-up of beings in the proper-forms of their subjective destinies. Perhaps destiny as something private, humble, and subjective can only be thought and historicized by means of conceits such as those we have briefly reviewed – conceits travelling directly from affectivity as such, needing no adequate emotion, affect, or relevance to be true.

The sense of subjective destiny as surreal idea and fixed form phenomenalizes itself pre-eminently in the firm outline of the notion of death. I have refrained from the facile act of viewing the figure-on-the-balcony image as a death-image, since such a reassuring notion conventionalizes other, more forceful, more Powys-specific, and more work-specific aspects of that figure; yet death too obviously looms on such a 'balcony' – as the narrator willingly recognizes. Running from the figure on the balcony is very much like running from the figure of death (590). Indeed the balcony-figure is intertwined with death through the fact that 'he' appears (for the reader and for Catherine) in conjunction with the death of Catherine's nurse. The deathwardness is explicit at one point: "What if it were her destiny after she died – as a punishment for loving one man and marrying another – to run like this by Rhisiart's side forever, through an eternal mist, towards a 'figure on a balcony' who eternally receded as they advanced?" (590). That which is 'after' death is simultaneously also deathwardness and death itself. To put the dead nurse "between herself and her life" is by the same token to put the figure on the balcony "between herself and her life" (590). Death as death-figure-on-the-balcony now overlooks an affective field in which death, without exactly splitting, without really dividing itself from itself, becomes its own double. This doubling-without-splitting in death is also a doubling-without-splitting in Catherine. Such doubling eventually runs through Rhisiart too. Upon breaking the news that she has purchased suicidal poison for Rhisiart and his fellow-prisoner, Tegolin finds that Rhisiart apparently needs to synchronize himself with some other being, his exact double. "Since he still remained inert and motionless, just staring at her with an expression as if he had to make sure that another Rhisiart, already in a different world, was correctly imitating him, she snatched at the phial" (834). Clearly "another Rhisiart" is a dead Rhisiart, a parallel Rhisiart living beyond life in a spirit world. But in so far as this other Rhisiart may be felt to be present rather than remote, his double is not really extraterrestrial, other-worldly, and transcendent, but closer to life than the 'regular' Rhisiart. There is a Rhisiart *on this side* of life, *on this side* of death-and-life. This immanent figure, in every respect more interesting than the traditonally-imagined supernaturalist double, is evidently at hand in the phantom 'presence' of Owen himself – hence the Prince's lack of interest in the conventionalized dialectic of life and death, absence and presence, victory and defeat, freedom and predestination. The word "inert" in the line informing us that Rhisiart remained passive and motionless (834) rehearses the sense produced by the word "amort" (600) in the earlier scene depicting the manner in which the Secretary "visualized the black figure alone on his balcony" (599). There, we may recall, the black slugs of Tywyn, living on the "under-side" of fallen leaves, living in fact "on their balconies," were instrumental in enriching the "mortuary smell" of the forest (600). It is clear, however, that even in this persistent death-atmosphere in *Owen Glendower*, the specific, surreal clairvoyance effectuated by the most acutely-wrought fancies is not at all reducible to death – not even when the idea of death goes hand in hand with the image that has been released from it. When we learn that Tegolin has purchased the phial of death-poison from an alchemist, and that this phial, "fastened round her neck by a long black ribbon" (833), lacks both colour and taste, we also come to know the words and the image used by the alchemist to identify the power of the poison in question: "'Death in thirty ticks of a *French* clock,' he said" (833). These ticks, precisely because they come from a *French* clock – rather than just any old clock – stand out from context in a strange manner. Yet this strangeness is not really sinister. There is a defiance in the idea that "the person would be dead in thirty ticks of a French clock" (833). It is as if the extraordinary nature of the poison – the distilled potency of its quality – belongs to the same degree of expenditure, renown, and shameless decadence as clocks made in France – indeed *ticking there.* But when Rhisiart voices his resentment at the expressive overkill in this seemingly nonsensical elaboration on the nationality of the death-clock, we have absolutely no way of knowing just what all the fuss is about. "Rhisiart replaced the stopper, laid the phial on its side on the third stool, and asked her with a certain irritation in his tone why it had to be a *French* clock. 'Can't we even take poison in our own way?' he said" (834). "French" needs to be taken ('taken' as in 'taking poison') in the way we take "candle-grease" (837), "straw" (836), and "click-click" (611) – as voiceless, unacoustic, 'unsemiotic' aberration; as something 'dropped' in history (as indeed in the work) by *itself.*

The word 'love' (much disliked by John Cowper) is in fact a clue to the emotional intelligence of these quaintly heterodox icons of imaginative truth. In Dickens, such 'love' is related to the affectivity of the child; but in Powys it is somehow not childish ...for the simple reason that it is not really human. The 'love' shown by the narrator for various items, 'words,' and beings is like the 'love' of a god – or of a prowling animal. This animal or animal-god is neither tame nor beastly. Its eyes move over language – over the ranges of its expressive possibilities – without any urgent sense of communicative functionalism ...as if the ones who are being addressed *will not pay attention anyway,* as if they will only halfheartedly direct a concentrated regard to the unlikely matters at hand.

In this context of 'love' one may wonder if it is possible to apply to the Powys-work the tender preoccupation with *things* typically demonstrated by the Powys-narrator. If such a critical move were possible, it would be necessary (in the manner recently sketched) to focus certain thingly spots in the artifact in their very thingliness only. We obviously get closer to the 'truth' about the poisonous death-ticking of a 'French' clock and to the truth about nuns kneeling in 'straw' by seeing such items of literary fancy contextually; but in addition we attain a quite different 'truth' about the actual experience of reading a work like *Owen Glendower* by *not* contextualizing the individual moment of vision – by letting it manifest itself in its moment *and nowhere else*. This sense that the life-moment is true only as a living showing of its pure insulation is crucial for the general building-up of atmosphere – and indeed of truth – in Cowperist romance. Consequently, and without any reluctance, the highest difficulty the work embraces is the challenging task of formulating a sense of history which, far from primarily depending on various 'developments,' depends on nothing at all. Such a 'history' is strictly speaking only true, accurate, when there is no 'flow' or onwardness. The essence of history, indeed of time, is insulation. To insulate is to be. To be is to insulate. 'Wales' is thus exemplary. Its historiography is its insulation. This historiographic insulation is not 'in' time ...but time itself. Insulation is history, the moment without context, the mound, forest, monastery or cave without horizon, without world. Time as insular moment is a non-conductor. The non-conductor, the moment of vision, prevents transfer of heat, meaning, sense, sound. Cowperism as insularism, as the visionary field of an over-hermit, secures its programmatic lack of acoustic broadcasting (polyphony/monophony) and of mundane semiosis precisely through this intermittent setting-up of non-conductors. These do not function in postmodernist fashion to create an overall sense of fragmentation. For there is no 'overall' sense in the first place. Insularity is thus not functional, and as literary vision insularism is not a programme or manifesto. The prevention of transfer from one moment of vision to the other is not the outcome of some ideological deliberation – but 'happens' just as history happens, just as time happens. There is simply that idea of the ticking French clock heralding death through poison. There is simply that figure on the balcony, that candle-grease on the stairs, those nuns kneeling on straw, those black slugs on the under-sides of the autumn leaves, those remarkable twitchings between the hazel eyes and the narrowly twisted chin of Prince Henry. *That* is history. Compared with these 'non-conductors,' the more consciously wrought disquisitions on the dialectic of 'up-and-down' and 'life-and-death' are trivial.

History, the arising of the moment as non-conductor, is a materialization of the insular, devoid of context. This essence of insular auto-affectivity is the 'I.' The 'I' does not 'flow' in time or history – but is on the contrary time and history *as such*; the moment as non-conductor. The ego 'flows' in time, 'develops' alongside the onward-moving 'forces' identified by historiographers. But the ego is not the 'I.' The 'I' is not onward-moving. Nor is it fabricated by 'forces.' It has no intrinsic reality other than itself ...and is strictly speaking not even an identity. In so far as the moment as insular non-conductor is an originary materialization of auto-affectivity, the life of this materialization is thus not the life of a 'person' but of the moment itself. But in the Powys world the moment is not primarily temporal. It is spatial. Time as insular non-conductor is space; but space is now no longer the three-dimensional, Euclidian space of classic representation but the ideative intimacy of auto-affection. A 'thing' in such non-Euclidian space is thingly by *not* being a representation, by not being 'in' space. The clumsy wooden image of Saint Clare is for Catherine no mere object. It is not 'something.' There is no 'otherness' in it, if by 'otherness' we refer to some quality bespeaking exteriority, alienation. It is important for us to recognize that the truly *felt* things in our lives do not belong to our 'surroundings' or to our 'representations' or to any other exteriority – but to affectivity itself, understood as auto-affectivity. Nor do the truly *felt* things of our lives belong to some supposed 'stream of consciousness,' some sort of elusive interiority which recedes inwardly as we reach introspectively for its essence. The truly *felt* things of our lives do not belong to world or to mind – but to feeling *itself*. Feeling itself does not 'flow' or 'stream.' It is neither exterior nor interior. As non-conductor, the clumsy wooden image of Saint Clare does not phenomenalize itself in Catherine's exterior or interior space. On the contrary, it phenomenalizes itself *as 'I.'* This phenomenalization of the clumsy wooden image of Saint Clare is a phenomenalization of *affectivity* in affectivity. The originary unity-lacking onefold, the originary identity-lacking not-twoness, of these 'two' phenomenalizations is feeling, the *Parousia*.

> [I]n their nervous excitement [Catherine's eyes] changed colour as often as Owen's did ...[She] solemnly crossed herself ...The breath of that April afternoon crept in through the unglazed window and lightly stirred the listener's fair hair. The misty sunshafts of the declining day had long since moved away to the westward; but their ruddy light, falling in a warm rich diffusion on the hill-side opposite, was countered, as the narrow window received its reflection, by a cavernous and mossy greenness, as if belonging to the interior of a cave, which hung about the heavily-pictured arras and about a clumsy wooden image of Saint Clare.
> This austere piece of carving, which was of life-size, had followed the girl from her nursery at Sycharth to her bower at Glyndyfrdwy; and it now stared forth with its cold virginal eyes towards the yet colder peaks of

Snowdon. (481-482)

This type of 'object' is more significant than the comet of chapter XIII. Moments of æsthetic, literary, and imaginative charm are produced by the sudden and unforeseen preoccupation with fancies of loved 'things' encountered more or less at random rather than by the various carefully-imagined details energized by sadism, supernaturalism, and other leading motifs of the work's blueprint. In fact it may be advisable at this point to call attention to a tension (without dialectic or polyphony) in *Owen Glendower* between two basic principles of organization: on the one hand (1) a sense of surveyability; on the other hand (2) a sense of non-surveyability. The first of these sensations (1) is given as an encompassing globalism achieved through multiple cross-references. These cross-references increase in frequency as the narrative progresses, culminating toward the end of the work in a mass of back-references (596, 605, 609, 670, 672, 682, 685, 696, 699, 739, 901-903, 908, etc). These events in which the work points back (or indeed forward) to its own already-realized reality create the impression of the tightness of a web, of the interlocking exactness of a jigsaw puzzle, of a causal nexus refined to the point of filigree. From the perspective of this narratological surveyability, 'history' is nothing other than the ready-made intricacy of this pattern. History is in the lap of the gods in the way that the unravelling of the quirks and meanderings of fiction is in the hand of the narrator. However, the equally significant sense of non-surveyability (2) produces a quite different, if not opposite, sense. The *summa* of the 'things' of history is not organizational in the first place – but unsurveyable to the point of mystagogy. Strictly speaking, no 'history' is manufactured by 'things' like the life-size wooden image of Saint Clare. There is a halo of 'non-historical' events, impressions, feelings, and beings around 'history.' Yet the encirclement manifested by this halo is not *felt* to be 'outside' history. Its mode of arising is not distance. Its situatedness is not horizontal. Its affectivity is not remoteness. History's halo is felt to be on this side of history. This feeling, the feeling of history's halo, is *there*, right there in the exterior facticity of the living moment *of history*. Once the significance of this halo has been recognized in *Owen Glendower*, we quickly also realize that its concrete, living materialization (in the reader, in the historical personage, even in the historical event itself) *is the condition of possibility for every other sense of 'history.'* Strangely, then, we cannot have any history, any historiography, without first having a halo of history – a halo of historiography. Now the inward halo of historiography in *Owen Glendower* has a substance: affectivity. This substance, affectivity, is a halo originating a history beyond history's ken.

Those free, pristine 'things' I have called 'non-conductors' (nuns kneeling on straw, stairs *sprinkled with candle-grease*, life-size wooden image of Saint Clare, clock ticking the last thirty *French* seconds of life) form a *summa* that is neither a sum total of beings and events surveyed by the godhead, nor a freeplaying exteriority in or beyond the 'margins' of surveyability. Instead the insularity of vision is such that its moment utterly defies every conceivable world-context. Without being the least platonic, ideal, or abstract, it is utterly non-mundane. Consequently, the accurate historiographer cannot permit historiography to mundanize such a moment of vision, for then it is *no longer historical*. The crux of historiographic matter, then, is that the observant regard which has assigned itself the task of tracking it down to the bare essentials of its phenomenological materiality must see it perfectly (with 20-20 vision) in the real-life insularity of its arising-realm and arising-manner. Since, as it happens, the feelings in and of history (as distinct from the feeling *for* history) arise *as feelings*; and since, moreover, feeling is essentially immanent *in its very materiality* (French clock, nuns on straw, grease on stairs), historical veracity may not be conveyed as knowledge about facts but only as initiation into feeling. History occurs in the world; but its materiality does not.

•

History is a real-life dispute about 'conditions,' a real material-political fight about rights and about accessibility; but the conditions, accessibilities, and rights are not void of affectivity. Nor have they become what they are without moving, in this very becoming-condition, becoming-right, becoming-accessibility, *through affectivity*. Against the background of such a contemplation of the materiality of history, one may ask in what way the writer's confrontation with the material brutality of war alters the rapport between artist and artifact. Does the act of writing a work like *Owen Glendower* force John Cowper Powys to modify the 'idealizing' tonality of his fiction – or can the cruel matters that are intermittently at hand somehow be assimilated within the Powys world as we have previously known it? This question can perhaps only be answered adequately by means of a prior move in which we ascertain exactly in what sense the Powys world is 'ideal' or 'idealizing' in the first place. The idea of the ideal is overtly thematized in the archetypal Powys novel. *Weymouth Sands* and *Maiden Castle* are almost unthinkable without the theme of Platonism and without the idea of a Platonic protagonist. *A Glastonbury Romance* is in its very essence a work that probes into the affectivity of the ideal. The Grail is nothing less than the ideal encountered in the moment of vision. The Grail is a *materialization* of idea – hence a 'thing' belonging in thematic tonality to the imagination of the Christian West. But in *A Glastonbury Romance*, the Grail as materialization of the ideal, the idea of the ideal *appearing as matter*, is by the same token the idea (indeed the concrete reality) of affectivity materializing ideatively as affectivity. Thus, ultimately, the Grail is affectivity as such, pure matter, affectivity as auto-visualized onefold. Affectivity is strangely material, and the Grail is nothing but an absolutizing of the self-materialization of affectivity. But misunderstanding should be avoided; there is not first something like affectivity, and then only subsequently something like a materialization. *Affectivity is matter from the outset.* Affectivity's materialization is originary. Matter 'is' beforehand affectivity. Affectivity 'is' beforehand matter. The school of thought investigating history based on such an originary reality would not be named 'historical materialism' but 'affective materialism.' Affective materialism, far from excluding the notion of 'idea,' needs to take it into account from the outset.

We see, then, that the event of investigating a supposed sea-change in the Powys world, one caused by a presumed reconsideration of reality's 'idealism,' is rather tricky. As Powys begins to totalize the material sense of physical war-cruelty, the material blow that shatters the idea of the ideal tends to idealize a new level of ideative affectivity no less 'idealizing' than the first one. When the page Elphin considers the manner in which a horrible war-sight may come to permanently jeopardize the way he idealizes a beloved lady-in-waiting, this intervening idea of shockingly material reality is itself presenced as an image carrying the potency and durability of an affective *idea*.

> There had been little resistance so far to the advance of the allies; but he couldn't get out of his head one Worcestershire hamlet where requisitioning had been opposed, and where they had left behind them blackened ruins, unburied bodies, wailing and cursing, and cries to heaven for vengeance.
>
> One horrible sight he had seen, a dead woman with a living child at her breast; and he found himself tormented by the thought that whenever in future he worked at his favourite subject of a unicorn surrounded by thousands of flowers some devil would force him to depict *that* woman in place of an idealized Luned! (807-808)

Here there is first an empiricist sense of material devastation. The ruins, bodies, and cries are empirical units in a world reduced to its naked, unsentimental, unideal materiality. But this dispersal-sensation is quickly drawn together by the fact that one further such empirical unit, the dead woman feeding her child, is a "horrible sight" that is intense enough to project itself *imaginatively* over endless time ("whenever"). "Whenever in future" ...this is a notion of time without limit. The "sight" is thus itself without limit. Moreover, this limitlessness is beforehand drawn into an ideal and idealizing landscape through the notion of a creative imagination working at the "subject" of its "favourite" preoccupation, a "unicorn surrounded by thousands of flowers." Inadvertently, the *idea* of a dead woman with a living child belongs ontologically to the imaginative field delimited "by thousands of flowers." There is an iconic energy at work, giving to the figure of the dead woman with her child an iconicity equal, if not superior to, that of the "unicorn." Unicorn and dead-woman-nursing-a-child conjointly shape an iconography in which symbols have become flesh, and in which flesh has passed ideatively from the incomplete materiality of war-objects to the richer materiality of war-objects seen in the glow of their affective domains. Such affective contexts are in fact already foreshadowed by the commentary informing us that "bodies" and "cries to heaven for vengeance" are co-originary. *In actual history*, the materiality of bodies and the materiality of feelings are not separate things. Feelings are not epiphenomenal. They are themselves originary, themselves just as material and actual as war 'itself.' There is in fact no such thing as war 'itself.' In war, there is already war-affectivity, and this war-affectivity is *affectivity*. In war, there are not first 'events' (events of 'history') and then, subsequently, affective 'effects' of such 'events.' The events themselves were affective through and through. The destruction of the hamlet and the killing of the mother were prompted by feelings triggered by the emotions of people who had "opposed" requisitioning (807). Only a superficial observer would decide to call all the war-events 'material life' and to call all the war-emotions 'subjective responses' to the events of 'material life.' In the actual flow of the historical materialization of war, no such academic cause-and-effect mechanism operates. The affectivity of war is just as originary (just as 'causal') as the events 'themselves.' The events themselves are never 'themselves.' They are always historical by being beforehand soaked in the real-life *materiality* of feeling. This materiality cannot, *qua* materiality, be separated from the iconography and iconicity of ideas. For ideas, in the Powysian sense, in the *historical* sense, are themselves affective, in other words material.

•

The general sense of the co-originary iconicity of ideas and affective materiality is manifested in the narrator's delicacy of touch in the matter of flowers, colours, and human defeats. To be in *Owen Glendower* is to be in a territory of flowers and flower-worship. To be in *Owen Glendower* is to be in a territory of defeat. To be in *Owen Glendower* is to be in a world of colours. These affective dimensions of historical romance do not simply lie alongside each other. They are not mere 'aspects' of content, of imagination, of literary achievement, of technique. They are expressions of a selfsame visionary comportment. This comportment has to do with magic. Colours are ideatively magical. Flowers are ideatively magical. *Defeats* are ideatively magical. The general affectivity of *Owen Glendower*, its essential *materiality*, is thus an encompassing sense of history as magic. There is something utterly unromantic about such a conception. For the 'romance' of a flower, of a colour, of a defeat is not something we add to 'it' – not something we may or may not choose to 'see.' There is in history itself, as soon as we give up our supercilious objectification of it, something magical, something that has got more to do with flowers, colours, and defeats than with 'a sense of history.' Those who have 'a sense of history' are somehow precisely those who are unable to be in history, to conceive it as life, indeed as matter. Are we saying, then, that suffering itself is magical? Are we saying that magic has something to do with suffering, with total human defeat? Perhaps we are.

The sense in *Owen Glendower* that individual suffering does not primarily belong to the individual but to suffering itself is a sense of magic. It is the sense that suffering is an extreme instantiation of the strict belonging-to-itself of feeling; but it is also a sense that *any* feeling, once it is self-totalized as feeling, is suffering. There is deep-suffering not only in pain but also in love, compassion, surprise, dreaminess, expectation, voluptuousness, relaxation, laziness, hope, sleepiness, euphoria, patience. A case in point is the account of the nimbus of Christian sympathy in which the narrator allows us to finally see even a disadvantageously depicted character like Father Pascentius. Whereas the reductions performed by the narrator are reductions of the world (in other words of representation) *to* affectivity, the reductions typically performed by this fat theological gentleman are reductions *of* affectivity – reductions of the affective materiality of life to the godhead. These theological reductions are "metaphysical." They are accompanied by a "metaphysical gesture, *reducing* all the changes and chances of this mortal life to the infinite indifference of the Absolute" (770; emphasis added). But although the narrator feels that this master of theology has misconceived, essentialized, and objectified the nature of the life of the spirit, he nevertheless permits Father Pascentius to effectuate a final exit that encourages us to view even *his* predicament as one of genuine self-suffering and genuine self-truth. Not only is there a part of Father Pascentius's life-presence that is absolutely authentic – because absolutely affective. (I am referring to his activity as a botanist devoted to the naming of rare, unclassified plants.) In addition, the very falseness of his self-consciously pompous behaviour is so false that it attains the affective potency of true emanation. Father Pascentius is true in his very falseness, absolutely true to his falseness. We *feel* Father Pascentius, his airy 'falseness,' as affective ideativity rather than as socio-ethical inadequacy. Any comportment that totalizes its own indubitable affect shows itself as *affective*. A compassion envelops the "pathetic figure" who is now dismissed from Glendower's court; but this compassion, rather than being a commiseration on the part of narrator or reader, rather than being self-pity on the part of the Father himself, is simply the manifest phenomenalization of the originary nature of feeling itself (770). Even the word 'compassion' is perhaps not quite intimate enough to identify the reality of the pure affective field in which the learned man is finally sighted.

> Father Pascentius, mounted on one of the castle's best horses and attended by two of the castle's sturdiest guards, not to speak of a baggage-mule loaded with the most precious books of the castle libraries, came jogging and swaying past them along the shore-road ...It would have needed the more sympathetic eye of Rhisiart to note the clumsy attempt of the man's plump fingers – entangled as they were with the reins he held – to make his familiar metaphysical gesture, reducing all the changes and chances of this mortal life to the infinite indifference of the Absolute.
>
> Let us hope that the tremendous shade of Saint Thomas himself noticed that blundering attempt of the hands that had composed the great Cistercian Commentary to bid farewell to Harlech with an appropriate gesture. Some of the most piteous things in life are these same brave whistlings and drummings and hummings wherewith, when our stars are crossed, we mechanically save our faces and cover our retreats; and those of us who feel tenderer to the weaknesses of an orthodox Scholiast than Owen

did may be permitted to hope that before getting very far on his road to face the toothless sarcasms of Chancellor Young the Father's roving eyes may light upon a wayside plant even more uncommon than the *Cardamine Pascentius*. (770-771)

On this side of the metaphysical zone of metaphysical gestures, *on this side* of the world, *on this side* of the sphere of representations, *on this side* of the space where the likes of Pascentius *represent* the 'Absolute,' *on this side of* the space where false materialists *represent* history as 'materiality,' in the area where the 'Absolute' (i.e. feeling) is *on this side* of a representation of itself, (being instead a feeling-of-itself, self-feeling as such without go-between) there is the possibility of a theology manifesting itself *on this side* of theology, *viz.*, botany. *On this side* of the metaphysical gesture we perceive the botanical gesture ...picking a flower, *naming* a flower. There is a botanical-theological affectivity that arises *on this side* of theology, a botanical-theological gesture that arises *on this side* of the gesture that represents itself, that gestures in representation, that 'waves' in the world. The fingers that are awkwardly entangled in the reins of retreat are the same plump fingers that perchance will need to pick a "wayside plant." The affectivity *of these fingers* does not really belong to theology, to history, or to man. It belongs to matter itself – to the finger, to the very slightness of 'botanical' movement, to movement as such in its unseen and unseeable reality. Such movements, the stuff and fabric of botanical intimacy but also the very stuff and fabric of John Cowper's historiography, are not mundane. History is always affective, but affectivity is not always historical.

2

WEYMOUTH SANDS

Weymouth Sands is a wonderful novel. In a sense it is the foremost work to come from the pen of John Cowper Powys. There is a sense of æsthetic consummation saving the novel from the sprawling excessivenesses of some of its chief creative rivals. *A Glastonbury Romance* has the same indomitable energy, and even the same type of internal happiness; but it does not have an equal sense of measure, poise, and economy. At the same time *Weymouth Sands* is not a curtailing of Powys's genius – in the way that *Great Expectations* sacrifices Dickens's marvellous capacity for nonsensical digression, demonstrated as early as *Pickwick Papers*. The lack of bulk and the loss of enormity do not prevent *Weymouth Sands* from asserting itself as mass. Weymouth is not less solid than Glastonbury. The advancing and retreating of sea-tides are not conceived on a scale that is more limited than the one utilized as canvas for the grand brushstrokes of history in *Owen Glendower*. In becoming John Cowper's most æsthetically perfect work, *Weymouth Sands* has made no sacrifices whatsoever. Here that which is most æsthetic is by the same token that which is most Powysian, most eccentric. For some strange reason, the eccentricity of *Weymouth Sands* is compatible with the principles of traditional æsthetic form – something which we can say of few other works from the hand of this artist.

John Cowper's best fiction and best philosophy is built on the idea – or indeed reality – of deliciousness. Deliciousness *as such* vanishes from the writer's horizon as he progressively slips from the height of his powers into old age. In this sliding, Powys drifts away not only from the astonishing precision of his material hold on the richness of his own life-receptivity but also from the idea of the work of art as a quintessentially Powysian construct. In John Cowper's best works, the idea of the presence of deliciousness is indistinguishable from the idea of the presence of amorous life. By amorous life I basically mean what the narrator means in *Weymouth Sands* when he describes the ideal-erotic affectivity of women like Gipsy May, Marret, and Peg Frampton as "a latent passion to offer up their amorous life as mystics offer up their souls" (272). In this assertion, 'amorous life' and 'soul' are understood as being on a par, as somehow being each other's possible substitutes. In other words, the 'soul' passes imperceptibly into 'amorous life' for a mystic who no longer lives in the ancient world of dogma but in the world as we know it today. In a sense, in fact, 'amorous life' is a refinement of 'soul.' 'Soul' cannot survive the onslaught of cynical modernity, but the 'amorous life' can. Whereas 'soul' is incompatible with mundanization, 'amorous life' is not. I am not suggesting that 'amorous life' is 'ideal' in the way that 'soul' is 'ideal.' In spite of the foregrounding of the amorousness of women as "erotic virginity" (272), the general steering of metaphysical attentiveness toward the idea of the "receptive" power of women is not an essentializing movement. The type of "essence" sought by Sylvanus Cobbold is "much more concrete" than anything dreamed by Platonists (271). "Essence" is an outcome of the event of "reducing the sensations of consciousness" (271). Impressions are beforehand precisely *affective sensations*. Affectivity in *Weymouth Sands* tends to be a "curious mystical contemplation" (271), and in the overall perspective of the work's total horizon, its reality as 'amorous life' is by no means something ideal. So by 'amorous life' I have something very large in mind. I have something in mind that is so big that it is not really confined to loving, to sex, or even to emotion. I have something in mind that is so absolutely all-important that it can be said to parallel the reality of the presence *of the sea*. For people in Weymouth, the sea is 'always there' whether they can see it or not, whether they can hear and smell it or not, whether they are thinking of it or not, whether it is 'there' or not. The same thing can be said of the amorous life. In Powys's most 'Powysian' novels, the amorous life is constantly present – present, that is, even when it is not mentioned, discussed, thematized, depicted.

Empirically speaking, there is much amorous life 'going on' in *Owen Glendower*, but the various love-games do not make up make up what I am presently calling 'amorous life.' 'Amorous life' may be provisionally defined here as a unique and special sense of presence. As the town Weymouth relates itself to the sea, so in Powys the literary work relates itself to 'amorous life.' 'Amorous life' is not something primarily empirical, this or that set of erotic adventures or misadventures. The amorous life is not something a narrator could thematize, objectify. It is not even something he can keep at a safe distance through internal irony. Hence the description of Sylvanus Cobbold as a man who takes the amorous life with "Don Quixote-like gravity and earnestness" (263) does not really open up a distance between the narrator and the amorous life – for the narrator is known to the reader, by now, as one who goes earnestly into the extreme limits of 'amorous life.' This lack of interval between the narrator and 'amorous life' cannot be rationalized. It is pointless to assert that there is a bit of John Cowper in Sylvanus or a bit of Sylvanus in John Cowper, for the 'amorous life' has ultimately got nothing to do with character, human life, or personality. It refers to itself, as the sea does. It can only be grasped on an æsthetic or ontological level. And grasping something on that level is not to grasp it but to feel it. The sea cannot be clutched, and 'amorous life' cannot be turned into one of the 'things' that appear in the artifact. It is rather that which makes the artifact possible in the first place. It follows, then, that the absence of 'amorous life' (in this special sense) in later works such as *Owen Glendower* and *Porius* – an absence for which 'history' is no viable compensation – is a withdrawal of the conditions that make the Powys world possible *qua* Powys world.

It may of course be argued that a lack of distance, far from promoting æsthetic truth, weakens it. Surely, as Kant and other æstheticians maintain, the very idea of art presupposes distance. Surely some withdrawal from immediate concerns is necessary as a condition for the birth of the materialization of something like an artifact. My reply to such an objection is that John Cowper's genius manifests itself as the ability to create an artistic 'object' *without* relying on any process of distancing. The evasion of distancing is effectuated in and through 'reduction.' A 'reduction' is a purification that permits something to contract transcendentally. Concreteness is thus not achieved through deployment in 'material' space but through a sense of "abstraction" (268) characterizing the affective materiality of the life of individual characters. In *Weymouth Sands* 'abstract' and 'concrete' are not opposites. The concrete presupposes abstraction in the way that the crystallization of the artifact as objectivity rather than subjectivity presupposes lack of distance (presupposes 'reduction') rather than distance. To detach oneself is to be in the material middle of life; to be sincere is not to sacrifice the æsthetic life, but to live it.

The 'reduction' I am referring to is nothing academic. It is no whim invented in order to promote interpretative ingenuity. Like Perdita Wane, most characters in this novel *feel* 'reduction,' its possibility or significance. "A strange, half-mystical detachment from all the poignancies and confusions of life stole over her; and she thought: 'Oh, if existence could be *reduced* to this – just looking at seaweeds and letting the world go!'" (175; emphasis added). Not only characters but the entire literary work undergoes 'reduction,' the work being ultimately nothing but the felt residuum that remains after 'reduction.' So I am saying that if one does not feel *Weymouth Sands* as reduction, and if one does not feel the phenomenological residuum – 'Weymouth' – as 'amorous life,' then one is not really reading *Weymouth Sands* but only some academic or commonsensical representation of it. A literary artifact, like any other artifact, is something felt, not just known. The event of feeling the artifact is nothing less than feeling it according to the drifting-energies of its idiosyncratic *self*-feeling. An artifact constantly feels *itself*; and I am saying that this self-feeling in the best Powys novels moves within the circumference of an encompassing affectivity, or sense of affectivity, which, following the narrator's own clues, I am calling 'amorous life.'

The expression 'amorous life' does not point to some sort of 'relation' between writer and artifact. I am not focussing on the 'love' that an artist may or may not have *vis-à-vis* the creative achievement. Nor am I in some Freudian way referring to the 'amount' of libidinal energy that the work is able to set free in itself or in the writer. We are not in the region of psychology or 'creativity' when we consider 'amorous life.' *Weymouth Sands* leads us to believe that life itself is 'amorous' – and that life is 'amorous' through and through even for beings who never come to know the thrills and pleasures of 'love.' The event of being "enamoured" (172) is by no means exclusively the event of being love-sick and romantic. It is rather the event of making an appearance in a territory – 'Weymouth!' – which in its very materiality is an *affective* reduction. As a result of 'reduction,' affectivity phenomenalizes itself *on this side* of the self. "That it should be himself, Magnus Muir, or rather that *nameless* hidden self, that was the self of all his secretest feelings, who was now actually holding this incredibly lovely being in his hands, seemed to him too exciting to be true" (127; emphasis added). The nucleus of affectivity is "nameless," because it is not 'Magnus' and not really 'self' either. Feeling appears as *feeling only*. It is "hidden," because it is not visible; *it cannot appear in the world*. Where can it appear then? In feeling, only in feeling itself. In this way, affectivity streams through all the world – while simultaneously having the strange property of not touching the world at all. Everything materializes in, as, and for feeling; yet this materialization, although it is more concrete than the world (more tangible, real, indubitable), is from any ordinary perspective of exterior or interior perception utterly abstract. The 'amorous life' cannot be 'internally perceived' (as the misguided psychologist may believe), for even the humblest act of perception requires some interval between perceiver and perceived. No such interval occurs in pure affectivity, in absolute feeling which feels only feeling as such. What I am calling 'deliciousness,' taking my cue from the narrator himself, is the felt certainty not merely of 'feelings' but of this purity and absoluteness. It is a mystical experience, in so far as the mystical understanding of life is a cancellation of all ordinary, commonsensical apperceptions of the nature of lived experience. Criticism's neutralization of the genius of John Cowper Powys begins with such an ordinary, commonsensical apperception – and systematically sets out to translate the Powys world right back into the order of reason. Such a translation-process inevitably begins with a misunder-standing of deliciousness, of feeling, and of amorous life. But if feeling cannot be 'internally perceived,' how could John Cowper 'perceive' it and then 'write about' it? Well, first of all, to write is not to perceive but to recreate. The act of recreating feelings, for instance those of childhood, may originate precisely in the fact that these feelings were never 'internally perceived' in the first place – and in the fact that they thus have no reality-in-the-world whatsoever until they are æsthetically recreated.

It is important to dismiss the view that works of philosophy are not artifacts, and of course also the parallel view that artifacts are devoid of philosophy. I recklessly assert that *Mortal Strife* is a work of art and that *Weymouth Sands* is through and through a major work of philosophy. But by 'philosophy,' I do not mean what the common understanding means. Nor does Powys. This is why the narrator expresses the view that philosophy is based on "purely emotional" cravings that lie "behind" its "exciting concepts" (98). These purely emotional "cravings" are "concrete and quite definite" (98). We are thus speaking of affectivity, of affectivity *as such* – not of the emotional but of the "*purely* emotional." Richard Gaul's "Philosophy of Representation" (100) is in point of fact not based on representation at all but on affectivity. His view of the word 'representation' is not based on the ordinary understanding but on the eccentric life-conception of the narrator and of numerous living characters in the novel – on the idea that life is ideally reducible, by means of an excited act of reduction, to concrete affective essences (97-99). The word 'representative' does not refer to the mind's ability to fabricate 'representations,' but to the fact that each unit of feeling makes an appearance in *two* places at once – one of them being situated in the world, the other being situated *on this side* of the world. It is this structure – and not at all 'polyphony' – that saves us from monism, from a Block Universe. The model, while being similar to the Platonic one, is in fact quite different. For the affective essences, although arrived at through abstraction, are themselves material-concrete – and the abstraction itself is affective. It is by means of an *affective reduction* that beings reach 'philosophy' ...but 'philosophy' by now means feelings. Indeed, 'philosophy' by now means *affective consummation*. By providing the reader with introductory information about Gaul's 'Philosophy of Representation,' the narrator is not performing some innocent portrayal of certain curious metaphysical ideas entertained by a solipsistic male character. The narrator is giving the reader crucial preliminary glimpses of a way of seeing life that runs through all beings in the work. Characters are free to enjoy units of possible affectivty on *both* sides of the line of demarcation running between the world and affectivity. This line is by no means the line of demarcation between objectivity and subjectivity, between reality and mind. For one does not arrive at life's material, concrete-affective essences by merely stepping back from external reality into the mind. The material essences (the feelings) are not given through introspection. Reduction does not mean introspection. It does not mean leaving the world in any ordinary way. It means having access to "some super-vision" (99), and having this access by means of a form of poverty. Richard Gaul "reduced his daily meals to two" (96-97). The poverty goes hand in hand with deliciousness. In sipping his tea and inhaling his cigarette-smoke, the philosopher of representation can enjoy the colourless greyness of the horizon-line in a mood where there is an awareness that sky and sea have been equally "reduced to the lowest possible level of emphasis to which any material phenomenon *could* be reduced without actually becoming invisible" (97). A "peaceful and soothing pleasure" (97) originates not only from the drinking and the inhaling but also from the reduction itself – from the sense that life is being digested at the purest (i.e most elemental) level of concrete abstraction, at the most absolute level of *material* idealization. To say 'concrete abstraction' is by now more or less the same as to say 'abstract concretion'; to say 'material idealization' is the same as to say 'ideal materialization.' The reduction has been taken *that* far. In the 'Philosophy of Representations,' the phenomenological residuum, the leftover remaining after reduction, is obviously that which is literally 'irreducible.' The 'irreducible,' we have understood, is affectivity ..."yearnings" that are "concrete, basic, *irreducible*" (99; emphasis added). These yearnings are not simply emotive (in the ordinary sense) but have to do with affectivity as such, affectivity being an originary amalgam of "intuition, instinct, emotion, and imagination" (99). A philosophical system is a "body of concrete palpable yearnings" (99), in other words an affective corpus. This is what the work itself is. This affective corpus, and not merely the sexual body, is our point of departure in the task of explicating the nature of the deliciousness of *Weymouth Sands* as amorous life.

•

Deliciousness, of course, is a feeling. "Breath after breath of incredible pleasure" fill Perdita as she perceives a great immobile heron standing in a glittering pool of water (167). The "emotion she felt" is to be understood as "a dark delicious trembling" that "surged up within her" (167). Such a delicious emotion does not always need to be positive. A certain type of thrill is a "delicious consternation" (141). Physical sensations may be delicious in their very negativity. When Daisy Lily perceives the chill of her cold night-dress, she has "a delicious shivering-fit" (85). More often, however, deliciousness is "a mild and dreamy satisfaction" (97), "a particular sweetness unlike anything else," a "vague, delicious feeling" (117). But if deliciousness is sometimes little more than a feeling, it is generally speaking not only that. As I have already pointed out, it has got something to do with 'amorous life,' and with 'amorous life' understood as something larger than 'human love.' I have also emphasized the importance of sea-presence for the phenomenalization of deliciousness as an *expanded* sense of 'amorous life.' In Weymouth, "the very breath and spaciousness of the blue sky and the distant sea" transform a walk into an expansive sense of "journeying through space" (123). "The shock of seeing so much of the sea at one view" may promote "a curious thrill" which moves the individual toward "a transport of delight" (100). We know that "such ecstasies" enable the "ecstatic senses" to live in a sense of "rapture" which by no means excludes the aforementioned "strange, half-mystical detachment" (174). It is precisely the detachment that completes the sense of enlargement, the stepping-back of the act of withdrawal being the material widening of the view that is at hand. This retreating-as-widening is paradoxical in the sense that it brings the affective *cogito* closer to the world as a place of material enchantment in the very act of withdrawing from that world. Perhaps the idea of the *wave* is important here. It retreats in approaching, approaches in retreating. Deliciousness is 'wavy' in the sense that the male succumbs to a "wave of intoxicating sweetness" in the presence of woman (121). Delicious waviness is not a wavering, not a hesitant coming-and-going of feeling. It is more like "an irresponsible feeling of well-being" (79). There is a lack of responsibility in the withdrawal from the world but also in the closeness to tangible materiality furnished by this very withdrawal.

The affective ideativity of irresponsibility is the material essence of the energy of the Powys novel. I am not referring to some flirtation on the part of the author with nineteenth-century decadence, or with twentieth-century decadence for that matter. I am not pointing the idea of 'irresponsibility' in the direction of morality but in the direction of affectivity. I am reviewing the event of 'irresponsibility' from the perspective of a criticism that understands itself as an analysis performed in the name of affective materialism. 'Irresponsibility' understood in the Cowperist sense involves a radical attitude of recklessness on the part of affectivity *vis-à-vis* its own lack of limits. Thus "an irresponsible feeling of well-being" (79) is a feeling of well-being and not something irresponsible. 'Irresponsibility' points to the absoluteness of the feeling that is at hand; and the absoluteness is the sheer indubitability in which feeling effortlessly and smoothly rolls through itself as feeling affecting feeling, as feeling feeling feeling. The self-feeling of feeling has nothing to do with a self. In feeling's feeling-of-self, feeling does not feel 'the self' but feeling. Here in a sense lies the riddle of 'irresponsibility.' It is utterly irresponsible on the part of feeling, and perhaps also on the part of the self, *not* to be the 'medium' through which feeling touches itself in establishing deliciousness. It is utterly irresponsible on the part of feeling to bypass all proper selfhood, to treat 'subjectivity,' the dull, everyday godhead of all 'respectable' bourgeois life, as nothing. The nonchalance of *Weymouth Sands*, of *Wolf Solent*, and of *A Glastonbury Romance* entails a prevailing defiance of "sluggish bourgeois common sense" (194). It entails a battle between one type of timidity, that of the bourgeoisie (195), and another. This other type of timidity, which by no means is excluded from the hearts of bourgeois beings, involves the kind of "mysterious happiness" that comes over most people in *Weymouth Sands*, including Rodney Loder (183). It is often based on "subtle and insubstantial feelings" – upon feelings which in their insubstantiality have the substance of the affective life. They permit the enjoyment of a deliciousness occurring in a "world within the world," the recognition of a "life within life" (183). As a sea-surface of affective truths and wayward visions, they make up the "essences" of a "deep day-dream" which takes its energy and life from "all manner of insignificant little scenes," scenes which gradually or instantly acquire "a sort of mystical value" (183). In *Owen Glendower* there is no such powerful defiance of sluggish sense but rather a sensation of a diplomatic compromise between the visionary life and plain existence. In many a writer, such a compromise may have its values – metaphysical, perhaps even æsthetic ones. But in the case of a writer who is as philosophy-dependent and as vision-dependent as John Cowper Powys the falling-away from 'irresponsibility' is æsthetically hazardous. What is left is not a narrator who has shifted his perspective but a discourse which only thinly disguises the simple fact that in it the narrator is partly missing.

It may be gathered, by now, that by 'narrator,' I mean, in the case of this writer's best works, no authorial 'voice' but deliciousness, irresponsible deliciousness. Although this deliciousness is at times confidentially voice-like in *Weymouth Sands*, this voice-like presence does not intrude as voice but as amorous presence. In *Owen Glendower*, by contrast, the narrator is sometimes a mere narrator, a 'subject' with all kinds of things to 'report' about history, humanity, existence, and death. This *narratorizing* of the narrator is an increasingly obnoxious factor in the later novels of Powys. There is generally speaking a *felt* difference between a work based on the sense of a narrator as amorous presence and a work based on the sense of narrator as narrator. The paradox is that a Powys work that insists on having a traditional narrator-as-narrator will be *felt* by the affectivity-oriented reader to be a work lacking a narrator, to be a work lacking 'amorous life.' In contrast, a work by Powys which, instead of using a personalistic narrator-figure, spontaneously utilizes amorous affectivity *as narrator*, will be felt to possess a narrator; and to possess a narrator 'who,' however much 'he' intermittently intrudes or fails to intrude, transparently inheres in the amorous onefold. Such a narrator, the *amorous narrator*, cannot participate in any 'polyphonic' interplay of interactive discourse-voices for the simple reason that he is far too affective, far too deep, far too sly, far too irresponsible, and far too wayward to want to participate in such a dull and bourgeois sense of artistic ingenuity. Such a timid sense of discursive entertainment originates in "the absence of a dominant imaginative passion" (107). I would suggest that despite much advertising deployed to suggest the opposite, *Owen Glendower* heads a string of 'works' that intermittently suffer from such an absence. These novels are not primarily children of passion but of work. The pre-eminence of passion over labour is at the heart of the life of amorous 'irresponsibility.'

There is plenty of ordinary amorous life in *Weymouth Sands* – the kind of sensational or non-sensational love-making we read about in evening newspapers. Enjoying some drinks with Adam Skald in the Weeping Woman, Perdita thinks it might be wise to "go as far as possible" while she has the chance (321). She would not mind becoming pregnant all at once; and *he* would not mind sleeping with her on the night before killing his enemy Dog Cattistock. Jobber Skald does not think of himself as altogether different from the "Margate murderer" – a man who has drawn the attention of the press because he has combined violence and sex in the way that sells newspapers. In this ordinary sense, 'the amorous life' is the "*furtivos amores* of middle class persons" (322). Its excitement is enhanced by "the conventional obstacles to free intercourse between the sexes" set up by the bourgeoisie (322). Empirically speaking, amorous life in *Weymouth Sands* is a depiction of the delights and embarrassments of such moments of social transgression. Amorous transgression of middle class life is symbolic of a general transgression of such life. The narrator slyly informs us that Magnus Muir enjoyed a "more than 'happy' quarter-of-an-hour" with Curly when he manages to briefly outwit the social humbug of her mother (316). With equal slyness, the selfsame narrator permits Curly herself to reveal her thoughts and reservations about "doing it," in order to exhibit her speculations about the required amount of transgressive violence that a man would need in order for her to "let him do it" (317). Clearly Magnus is not really up to this. Consequently there comes to view for Curly the rather more enjoyable image of the ardent love-making of young Sippy Ballard; Magnus's "dalliance" carries her imagination away "to her seducer's bolder usage" (317). "'Sip, oh, Sip! if it were *you*, my sweet Love, my clothes would be off me before I could say –' And she made a protesting, endearing, girlish little click with her tongue, as if she actually felt her frock slip to the ground" (317). Here transgression (the amorous recklessness of a middle-aged tutor) is itself transgressed – Curly Wix overstepping the sexual limits set up by Magnus Muir in the very act that confirms our sense of Muir as a violator of social norms. This sense of sexual violation is in its turn harmless compared to the one that is deployed around Dog Cattistock – a man of action who is so calculating in his drive to power that he stages a risky life-saving swim in the middle of a night-storm not just in order to give his agitated employees a demonstration of his civic superiority but also in order to drive his mistress to the extreme limits of sexual madness. "She'll love me tonight as no woman has ever –" (287). His reputation as "a Cro-Magnon" or "plain brute," far from turning his future wife off, turns her on. "Well *that's* what 'Tensia likes!" (296). But even within the timid sexual aggressiveness of Magnus Muir there dwells this selfsame brutishness, the only difference being that what *he* would "do" to Hortensia would be somewhat more gentlemanly and æstheticized. It "struck Magnus that if he were Cattistock he would get pleasure from ruffling back that hair with his fingers, from that lovely white brow!" (297). Magnus's tendency to co-imagine the erotic act and the reprehensible 'scientific' act of torturing dogs points to the fact that in him the 'amorous life' is no less *violently* transgressive than in the plain brute (307). His transgressions of middle class limits manifest his inability to surpass those limits and that class.

It is clear, then, that there is a narrator – and indeed a sly one – who is intermittently permitting us to peep into the little triumphs and shames of amorous heroes. *This,* however, is not what I mean by the 'amorous narrator.' The amorous narrator is not a personlike being. He is not someone who ushers us into certain delicate scenes, situations, and pleasures. The amorous narrator is not altogether different from "an Absolute that saturated with itself certain concrete objects more than others" – an Absolute consisting of the "minute particulars" of our "own lives" (323). Such an Absolute is not classic, not "Parmenidean" (323). For Sylvanus it has got to do with "a simple, direct, categorical way of living upon the earth" (324). I dismiss utterly the objection that this centring of an 'Absolute' is not central to the work but only to one of its characters – Sylvanus. That kind of remark is insensitive to the fact that *Weymouth Sands* phenomenalizes itself as affectivity, and that affectivity phenomenalizes itself as 'amorous life.' The work does not slip in and out of the philosophies of Sylvanus Cobbold, Magnus Muir, and Richard Gaul in the way that it slips in and out of the viewpoints of Dog Cattistock, Curly Wix, and Sippy Ballard. Rather, the 'philosophers,' without exactly being spokesmen for the 'philosophy' of 'the writer,' are essentially in tune with the work as a visualized affective totality. The word 'totality,' like the word 'Absolute,' is out of fashion. But frankly I do not care. *Weymouth Sands* is a totality – and it is a totality in the sense that the *sea* is an 'Absolute.' This point is made, and made with philosophic self-consciousness, in the very opening words of the book. "The sea lost nothing of the swallowing identity of its great outer mass of waters in the emphatic, individual character of each particular wave. Each wave, as it rolled in upon the high-pebbled beach, was an epitome of the whole body of the sea, and carried with it all the vast mysterious quality of the earth's ancient antagonist" (17). That there can be swallowing totality without any restricting sense of exhaustive totalization, that totality and inexhaustibility are not mutually exclusive – this is what the sea makes us feel, makes us know, and makes us *see*. The "minute particulars" cannot be extracted from the totality – cannot be 'detached' from 'Weymouth,' from the co-presence of the sea, from the 'Absolute,' from the amorous life. Rather than being units 'within' the Absolute, they *are* this Absolute. It is this sense of the vanishing of any discrepancy between 'Absolute' and 'objects' (323), between 'Weymouth' and Clock-Statue-Nothe-Spire, that makes the 'Absolute' *absolute*. This, and nothing else, is the affectivity of the 'Absolute.' During an encounter in the Weeping Woman, Jerry Cobbold calls attention to the fact that in the perceivable sound of the sea there is something not only reassuring but *absolutely* reassuring. In the Weeping Woman, the perpetual presence of the sound of the sea "makes you feel as if you were in a ship" (327). Jerry reminds Sylvanus of their time as children playing in an old training-ship. Jerry used to be scared by the noise of the gurgling water outside, but Sylvanus used to say "It's only the sea." This idea tranquilized Jerry. "That quieted me. 'Wherever it flows,' [Sylvanus] said, 'it's always the same sea!' ...I've often thought of that when life's got me by the hair. 'It's always the same life'" (327). This idea of the self-sameness of the sea and of the selfsameness of life – in other words this idea of the 'Absolute' – far from being simple is utterly elusive. In fact one might view the entirety of *Weymouth Sands* as nothing other than an enduring imaginative and artistic meditation on this very difficulty. For 'selfsameness' here is not a commonsensical selfsameness, not the kind of selfsameness that the academies interpret in classic fashion as identity and hence as an opposite of difference. The 'selfsameness' of the sea, and hence of life, is not logical but *affective*. No one living on the this planet can *not* perceive the sea as 'selfsameness.' No one on this planet can *not* perceive the affective selfsameness of the sea as the affective selfsameness of life. Of course the word 'life' is tricky, for if 'life' is narrowly understood in logico-classic fashion as empirical existence, one cannot speak of any 'selfsameness' of life. By 'life' in such an assertion we must be referring to affectivity, indeed to auto-affectivity. This is why Sylvanus quickly objects that "'Jerry's wrong when he says it's *life* that's 'always the same'" (327). Something is "'always the same.' "But it isn't *life*, brother'" (327). In Sylvanus's terminology, 'life' is not transcendental (i.e. affective, real). That which is truly real is "beyond" the life-and-death dimension (328).

The 'Absolute' is saved from metaphysics, from the academies, from 'Parmenides,' by absolutizing itself as affectivity rather than as a fantastic superconstruct. Affectivity, in so far as it is auto-affectivity, effortlessly *absolutizes* itself. In a sense this absolutizing is devastatingly simple. It means that a thrill is absolutely that which it is. That a feeling, say of a colour, a line on the horizon, a bird, is nothing short of perfect. Each feeling felt in the pure releasement of its own affectivity is the feeling it is, and it is this feeling-itself *absolutely*. There is no fissure, interval, internal distance, or hiatus. Nothing separates feeling from itself. *Weymouth Sands* foregrounds characters who everlastingly suffer from the fact that the feelings they have – whether pleasant or unpleasant, whether desired or undesired, whether tranquilizing or agitating – are indubitable. Characters in *Weymouth Sands* face the fact that, in life, feelings are exactly what they are. In many academies, thousands of over-intellectualized illusions and superstitions about the nature of feeling circulate. Feelings are said to be deferrals, estrangements, alienations, gaps, intervals, differences, spacings, and distances. In life, however, this is not so. *We feel what we feel.* And we feel what we feel absolutely. Even half-feelings are felt absolutely, precisely as the complete, indubitable sensation: this is a half-feeling. To live on earth is to be unable to deny the fact that you are having the feeling you are having. When you are sea-sick, you cannot truthfully understand yourself as not being sea-sick. If life is affectivity, life is absolute. If life is absolute, affectivity is auto-affectivity. Sea-sickness is not *ultimately* produced by the sea, but by the fact that affectivity can receive itself, and do so absolutely.

John Cowper Powys's important works foreground an event I shall call *affective consummation*. This is often a micro-event, an insignificant episode triggered by the remote noticing of an elusive detail in an object, person, landscape, word, emotion, thought, idea, or movement. Such an affective detail is absolute. Such an affective detail is *the* Absolute. The 'Absolute,' then, is feeling, detailed feeling, feeling-a-detail, the affective-occult details of feeling as such. In this feeling-of-details, the 'Absolute' knows itself as 'Absolute,' and it 'comes' to this knowing as feeling. The *absolute detail* feels itself. The self, or pre-self, in *Weymouth Sands*, is nothing other than this feeling-detail as absolute self-feeling. The self does not have to go around 'feeling' itself in order to be absolute. Instead it suffices to live by the sea. To live by the sea – this is not to 'have' an amorous life. It is to *be* amorous life, and to *be* amorous life in every detail of life. To *be* amorous life in every detail of life is to *be* absolutely and to *be* amorously. Each detail of amorous life is absolute, but each absolute detail of the amorous life does not have to be amorous, if by amorous we refer to some sort of love-making.

I refute all theories of 'desire,' 'seduction,' 'libido,' and 'the body.' I am not theorizing about a presumed sex-energy which supposedly explains everything from computer-language to chimney-pots. I am stating something that is utterly irrefutable: that in *Weymouth Sands* as well as in life feeling arises as that which cannot be denied. The one who has a certain powerful feeling on Saturday at 7.30 pm and who at 10 sharp on the following Sunday morning tells himself or herself that this feeling was not 'true' is a self-deceiver. All feelings *that we have had* are true, even the so-called false ones, even the ones we retrospectively rationalize as fallacious on the grounds that such handy revision preserves our life-illusion and our self-respect. The *words* we have at our disposal may or may not be true with respect to our feelings. "As [Sylvanus] kept murmuring and muttering about the 'Absolute' it was perfectly clear to both Peg and Marret that the feelings he described were rather obscured than revealed by the words he used" (323). But if the words for our feelings may waver with respect to the feelings, these feelings cannot waver with respect to themselves. Even a 'wavering' feeling is precisely that – a wavering feeling. When affectivity is wavering, it cannot assert that it is not wavering. When I am madly jealous or terribly bored, I cannot in truth assert that I am not jealous, not bored.

•

We are now on the verge of stepping into an issue of centremost hermeneutic significance – the question of the status of ambiguity in *Weymouth Sands*. For just as absoluteness and inexhaustibility refuse to cancel each other out in this work, so too do absoluteness and ambiguity. We may therefore speak of something I will call *absolute ambiguity* – by which I do not refer to some sort of ambiguity that has gone berserk, to some sort of ambiguity that has lost its head and become 'superambiguous.' I refer instead to the felt reality of something that might be called *ambiguity as Absolute*. That is what 'Weymouth' is. *Weymouth Sands* understands Weymouth as 'Absolute.' But *Weymouth Sands* also understands Weymouth as ambiguity. There is no distance or interval between these two understandings. They are a onefold without unity, a selfsame *feeling* without self-identity.

The ambiguity of absoluteness and the absoluteness of ambiguity may be understood by considering religion. The phenomenalization of religious feelings is crucial in *Weymouth Sands* – and by that I do not refer to the banal fact that certain characters, like Sylvanus Cobbold, are religious or pseudo-religious. In an important sense, and despite much internal irony suggestive of the reverse, *the best works of John Cowper Powys are religious through and through*. The cynical-secular Rabelaisian obscenity of John Cowper's intellectuality leads many a reader to believe that the writer has entirely disconnected himself from Christian sentiment and indeed from religious affectivity in general. Nothing could be less true. Far from being 'less' religious than the so-called Christian writers of æsthetic modernity, John Cowper Powys is more so. It is precisely here that we can begin to come to terms with the idea of the 'Absolute,' the idea of 'ambiguity,' the idea of 'amorous life,' and the idea of 'sea.' I am reluctant, here, to go along an equally fallacious path – the one that skirts the question of religious feelings by focussing on the Powys figure's affectivity in terms of 'hedonism' and 'stoicism.' It is futile to attempt to understand the affectivity of the Powys hero on the level where it is superficially advertised, on the level, that is, of nature-enjoyment and girl-enjoyment. For the Powys figure is not really enjoying nature or girls but the ambiguous halo of feelings that materialize in amorous situations and amorous environments. By the religious sense of the 'Absolute' I do not mean the infantile objectification of the godhead as a supernatural being exterior to the ongoing ambiguity of affectivity. Rather, in alignment with clues provided by Eckhart, I conceive the absolute simply as affectivity, as the appearing of affection in itself. The 'Absolute' is nothing other than the pure self-affecting of affectivity. 'Weymouth' is the sea affecting *itself*. How does it affect itself? As 'the sea,' as religion, as absolute, as feeling. 'Weymouth' is 'amorous life' affecting itself. How does 'amorous life' affect itself? As absolute ambiguity. As ambiguity affecting ambiguity. Ambiguity is absolute. This is the halo. Life is "a substance that resembled mother-of-pearl" (212)

A pearl is at once ambiguous and absolute. It is a 'vague' solid. But so too is 'Weymouth.' So too is the "pearly expanse" of the sea (303). The "undulant mass" of its "opalescent water" permits the one who lacks an amorous life to swim in affectivity as in amorous life (303). The chastity of Ruth Loder does not debar her from the affective immanency of a "sea-atmosphere" that brings her life into the intensest "magic of Eros" (303). Her indifference to men is that which allows something else to be felt as something that "slid into her." "Something" from the sea, "from that empearled surface," touches the quick of "her deep-rooted nervous system" (302). But whereas in *Owen Glendower* such a nervous system is sometimes understood primarily as precisely a system of nerves, in *Weymouth Sands* it is conceived instead as a presence affecting itself – like the sea – and *being what it is* in this very self-affecting. For this reason, "the pearly shimmer" is not primarily a feature of nature that 'affects' someone's sensibility – but absolute affectivity effortlessly affecting itself beforehand, absolute affectivity affecting a floating, concrete (i.e. felt) immanence which is at one and the same time feeling and sea, sea and feeling, opacity-transparency and transparency-opacity. As "some tremulous substance more stable than water and more vaporous than glass" (302), that which mediates the feeling of 'Weymouth' ...*is this feeling* ...'Weymouth,' 'amorous life,' mist, the sea. That which mediates and that which is mediated are a selfsame sea-atmosphere, air-atmosphere, landmark-atmosphere, perhaps even love-atmosphere. That which is mediated by affectivity is affectivity. That which is mediated by 'Weymouth' is 'Weymouth.'

•

The difference I am calling attention to between a 'set of nerves' and affective presence does not originate in the fact that the reader or the narrator entertains "romantic sensations" for "the presence of the sea" (171). By 'presence' I am not referring to the empirical availability of something felt to be 'present.' I am not even referring to an object that could be 'transcendentally' present "in a trance of adoration" (171). It is not some "poetical sensuality" (170) that permits me to *feel* 'presence.' The condition of possibility for such an absolute-ambiguous event is rather the underlying sense of having something all to yourself. This sense of having something all to yourself has nothing whatever to do with selfishness, with self-absorption, or with so-called self-indulgence. For in this work we can without any sense of strain assert that Weymouth has the sea all to itself. The landmarks 'have' each other because Weymouth *has itself* absolutely. This absolute self-having is not a self-possessing but a losing-of-self-in-affectivity, a losing-of-self in ...'Weymouth.' "Why was it that the happiest moments" in Rodney Loder's life "were when he had Spy Croft entirely to himself"? (182) In the Powys world, having something entirely to yourself means not that the self utterly holds itself to itself but that, *on this side* of this very self, *affectivity* has itself to itself. This affectivity, although it is *on this side* of the self, is not 'within' the self, not buried in some sort of 'subjectivity' – but just as much 'beyond' selfhood as 'this side' of it. The transcendental is absolute-and-ambiguous *because* it has no locus. Not only does it have no fixed locus – it lacks locus altogether. It is in this sense that we feel that the sea itself lacks situatedness. The sea *as such* is never in a certain 'place.' Looking at the sea in one place is looking at the sea in all places – it is to have a gaze that *feels* the inexhaustible totality of all sea-places.

That Weymouth has the sea entirely to itself, this is a feeling. In the men and women of Weymouth it is a deep daydream. The deep daydream is not a unit of subjectivity, it is not specifically human. Hence the landmarks too dream this dream – by day, and indeed also by night, as suggested by the awakened eyes of the figure of the Sea-Serpent during the night-storm. The "logos" (308) of the novel is the dreamy entirely-to-itself feeling. The logos is buried in an origin distant enough to elude the reaches of discursive articulation. A "kind of aura of it hung in the air" (308). As such a halo, this logos has the affective quality of the thought of 'wet' sand (308). The logos-halo, as a *wet halo*, is saturated by the sense of 'Weymouth' as Weymouth-having-itself-entirely-to-itself. The logos, the halo, the 'wet' sand – each has itself entirely to itself. But the self-havings are blurred into each other. The pure blurring is not a loss of individuation but an affective immersion in the overall 'wetness' (absolute æsthetic ambiguity) of the literary vision. This vision, as in the substance of the most rarefied and 'humid' colorations of Watteau, has the misty quality of soft revelation. The affective citizens of Weymouth seem to be perpetually within the reach of such a vaporous hallucination. The revealed hallucinatory object is more often than not the force of hallucination itself – a power which the narrator acknowledges as a truth-source rather than as a distortion of correct vision. The physical reality of vapour as a mist-phenomenon that "softened and blurred" the "orb" of the sun (118) is by implication religious (in the aforementioned sense). In the Lodmoor flats, the half-idiot Larry Zed is no less in touch with the 'religious' entirely-to-itself affectivity than any other being breathing within the 'logos' of absolute ambiguity. He sees what each being ought to be able to see. He actually *sees affectivity*. This *seeing* of affectivity as such, far from being a semi-religious event, is religious life in its most concrete and absolute (i.e. ambiguous) form.

[I]t seemed always to be his destiny to experience this awareness when his mind was particularly disturbed. But he stopped today on the crest of the pebbles and gave a deep groan of wonder; for the dawn-mists from the marshes had broken into troops and squadrons of ghostly figures, who, as they swept away over the sea, dissolved into thinner and thinner vapour, until they melted into nothing at all; and it struck Larry's mind ...as if some phantom Jesus, followed by all his disciples, had decided to perish in the waves. (136)

•

Sylvanus Cobbold views the 'Absolute' as something 'behind' life (328). Yet although such an idea is frequently foregrounded in *Weymouth Sands*, it is perpetually undermined not only by far less conventionalized forms of mystico-religious affectivity but by a generalized apperception of the fundamental absurdity of looking for essences 'behind' phenomena. Jerry Cobbold rejects his brother's transcendent outlook: "Behind ...behind ...behind – that's where you tricky mystics always put the secret" (328) – and this remark, far from just signalling a contrariness between brothers, points to a fundamental intellectual Powys-sensation: essences are not 'behind' phenomena; on the contrary, phenomena *are* these very essences. *Phenomena are essences, essences are phenomena.* In a strange way, however, one must perhaps move slightly 'behind' phenomena in order to recognize *that* this is so. In this way, what seems to be a vacillation on the part of the narrator, or indeed on the part of the work, between two altogether different conceptions of phenomenalization – one traditional-platonic and one radical-phenomenological – is in point of fact no vacillation at all. The work's 'blurring' of the 'Absolute' is at once hyper-complex and straightforward. The Weymouth 'Absolute' is in a sense much *more* straightforward than any 'Absolute' hailed by conventional religion, than anything sighted by "unctuous religiosity" (347). The Weymouth 'Absolute' is more straightforward *because it is phenomenon.* Yet the ambiguity of the phenomenalization of this phenomenon, the diffused-affective nature of its concreteness, blurs the straightforwardness, creating something like a 'blurred straightforwardness.' 'Blurred straightforwardness,' far from being something academic invented by criticism to baffle the intellectual public, is something physical and real turning up everywhere in the text. 'Blurred straightforwardness' characterizes sea-phenomena in 'Weymouth.' Since the sea is 'Absolute' in *Weymouth Sands* – being not only itself god but also the "watery floor which the sea-god...crossed" (352) – all sea-phenomena are 'absolute' phenomena. Such absolute phenomena *are* the 'Absolute'; but they are an 'Absolute' which appears as blur, as an "effect of elemental opacity" (352). This opacity, which itself is absolute, which itself is *the* 'Absolute,' is immensely enlarged (through auto-affectivity) *by itself.* Hence 'Weymouth' – in other words the 'Absolute' – is not merely aqueous ...but "terraqueous" (353). But this, the terraqueous as 'Absolute,' is by the same token the 'amorous life.' This does not simply mean that "the most absolute" (353) love-encounters occur terraqueously – on a sea-ledge, culminating in a ritualistic co-digesting of sea-holly (355-356), in a sort of terraqueous communion. Nor does it simply mean that the absolute godhead is a "sea-god" in the sense of "an immensely enlarged" lover (352). The terraqueousness of 'amorous life' is rather the elemental auto-ambiguity of affectivity in general and as such. After considering his just-completed possession of Perdita Wane, Jobber Skald says to himself: "It's God!" (358). "It" here is absolutely ambiguous – and the narrator's offhandish rationalization of "God" as the Jobber's "life-illusion" does not clear up the ambiguity at all. Such an attempt to lessen the absolute ambiguity is futile for the simple reason that any lessening of the ambiguity would be a lessening of "God." The idea that the 'Absolute' is experiential, that it is connected with "his uttermost life-sensation," is no more helpful than the idea that it is interpersonal, a "new Being that was them both" (358). Such explanatory comments take nothing away from the work's overall sensation of life as auto-ambiguity, of auto-ambiguity as terraqueous opacity, and of terraqueous opacity as an all-inclusive, inexpressible happiness animating not only lovers and 'happy' beings but also the most miserable and 'lost' creatures of sea and land. The name 'Perdita' is itself attuned to this affective opacity, 'loss' being itself lost in absolutely ambiguous configurations of terraqueous hope.

To be "god-like, cosmogonic" (353) in *Weymouth Sands* is not to be supernaturally high and mighty but rather to be ambiguous. As absolute, such opacity can phenomenalize itself in transparency. This opacity-as-transparency is the defining quality of *halo*. A halo is clear because it is opaque. It is opaque because it is clear. Effortlessly, the absolutely opaque appears to itself as absolutely opaque. There is no opaqueness (phenomenalization-effort) between the opaque and itself. *Vis-à-vis* itself, without any internal strain (internality is lacking in the first place), ambiguity is transparent, absolutely devoid of all mystery, absolutely known. Perdita and Adam Skald know each other precisely in this sense – they know each other absolutely because they are without effort each to the other utterly opaque. The narrator makes this point on numerous occasions throughout his account of their climaxing rendezvous. Auto-ambiguity is in this way the transparency of terraqueous ambiguity to itself. Although Perdita and the Jobber *have no secrets* (to permanently hide from each other), the one is to the other an utter mystery. This fact that the one is a complete mystery to the other does not prevent them from living in a realm where no mystery intervenes, or *can* intervene, between two mutually enamoured beings. In the light of this strange phenomenalization of the opaque-transparent halo-affectivity, I understand the most significant nature-descriptions in *Weymouth Sands* not as descriptions 'of nature' at all. When, during the course of the sea-ledge rendezvous, the narrator informs us that the western sky has been turned by the afternoon sun into something that phenomenalizes itself as "one piece of unbroken gold-leaf" (352), I view this assertion not as information about certain meteorological conditions passed on to 'the reader.' I understand such an assertion as a contribution to a constantly ongoing fabrication of an encompassing sense of the nature of affective reality. What is being described is not first of all the sky but the way in which life is phenomenalizing itself as *affective* life – for the lovers, but of course also for 'Weymouth,' for the religious-æsthetic totality. The "unbroken gold-leaf" is a materialization of the affectivity of auto-ambiguity; a materialization in which matter is opaque *in* its transparency, transparent *in* its being-opaque. Such a shimmer arises out of the fact that feeling always is two absolutes at once: pure invisibility and pure evidence. Any manifest feeling is for *itself* something absolutely invisible *in* the act of being absolutely evident. The self-evidence of feeling is its invisibility, its 'transparency.'

I have always asked myself why I find the nocturnal, slow-moving manifestation of a long procession of small white clouds (364) to be the most beautiful and moving phenomenon in *Weymouth Sands*. Perhaps this has to do with the sense of the nocturnal itself – understood not as obscurity but as auto-transparency, as the clairvoyant showing of the invisible (the unseen, Night) to itself. The long procession of small white clouds marches slowly over the stone roof of the Sea-Serpent's Head several hours before dawn. The lovers and the people asleep in the Sea-Serpent's Head never see these small clouds approach, pass overhead, and finally disappear at the other end of the sky. The account of the train of small white clouds moves us because we are given the sense that *no one* is there to feel them – and because the reader, *as* this no-one-there-to-feel-them, is at once a substitute for the missing receiver of night-sky affectivity *and* the 'no one' *feeling does not need* in order to be that which it is. I am referring to this specific cloud-feeling but also to feeling as such and in general. On a simple level of interpretation, one might say that 'the reader' sees (and therefore feels) what Perdita and the Jobber cannot see or feel. But it would be a mistake to believe that this nebulous entity 'the reader' is merely a personalistic entity, the affective middleman 'between' sky and sleepers. *Weymouth Sands* promotes no such narrow sense of affectivity as an empathizing go-between. Rather it is suggested throughout the novel that feeling requires no go-between. The hush and muted serenity of the cloud-procession point to the radical superfluity of the go-between in the realm of affectivity. Feeling needs 'no one' and 'nothing' to feel itself. (Feeling's empty middle is a 'no-between' rather than a 'go-between.') In this sense the 'no one' or 'no-between' *that feels* the long procession of small white clouds passing overhead at night is in a curious sense neither reader nor narrator but feeling itself. On account of love-passion and murder-passion, Perdita and the Jobber are no longer personalistic world-figures. In so far as they live in the communion of feeling itself and as such, in so far as they *are* this communion rather than two mundane egos, the lovers belong to the generalized affectivity of the Sea-Serpent's Head ...so that in an important sense they share in this long procession of small white night-clouds right at the moment of their slowly-moving phenomenal materialization. The image of 'Melia and Celia "stirring" in their sleep and murmuring "confused and troubled nonsense" (365) is one of the work's many explicit and implicit references to *Macbeth*, a drama which of course itself explores the nature of affectivity as auto-affectivity. Sleep is no doubt the most obvious instantiation of affectivity's self-referentiality, being the mode in which one can witness feeling's capacity to phenomenalize itself only, to radicalize a sense of consciousness without world. In this larger perspective, the 'eyes' in the 'Head' of the Sea-Serpent – mostly closed, sometimes wide-awake during storms – call attention to an agitation in affectivity which, by actually being nothing other than an auto-agitation, is in the final analysis reassuring ...like dream-sleep itself. The love of Perdita and the Jobber is essentially in attunement with sleep, even during the agitations of insomnia. So the general feeling of that slow procession of small white clouds is not that there is some importantly-felt 'contrast' between the sublunary plots of mankind and the tranquility of the heavens, but that the lovers, in the very wakefulness of their love-quarrel, sleep in one another in the way that sleep moves across sleep, in the way that the sky moves *across itself,* as sleep. There is a procession of something across itself. The stillness or tenuous nothingness of this self-traversing is ...'amorous life.'

The 'no one' or 'no-between' that feeling requires in order to be itself is 'Weymouth.' The pervading sense that Weymouth is *animated,* sometimes supernaturally self-quickened, is thus not really derived from some underlying occult sense of unknowable superlife; for even a reader who is utterly hostile to the idea of the extraterrestrial and supernatural is able to fully *be* in the auto-animism of 'Weymouth.' Such animism is derived from feeling itself. It is derived from the overall sensation that life is an auto-animating of feeling by itself. The tautological surplus yielded by such auto-animation builds a sense of life as something moving constantly out into the circumference of its own halo but also a sense of a satisfaction great enough to disallow any overstepping of this circumference. Any desire to 'go beyond' the outer limits of a halo is by definition absurd – since the 'outer limit' of a halo is no spatial-geometric line in the Euclidian world of rational representations but rather a spontaneous recognition in feeling of its own material-essential 'rotundity,' of its delight in being uniformly equidistant not from itself but from its own vanishing.

The idea of the auto-animation of feeling as auto-affectivity may create the false impression that feeling in Powys is in essence solipsistic. Nothing could be less true. This is why the thematization of vivisection is no mere contingent element in *Weymouth Sands* – no mere cursory reference to some 'exterior' reality that intermittently impinges on the work's central concerns, supposedly those of introspection devoid of compassion, altruism, and alterity. The fact that the 'halo' knows no 'beyond' does not mean that this selfsame 'halo' ('Weymouth') ignores the life and suffering of 'the other.' Nor does it mean that this 'other' is somehow 'included' in the 'halo,' in auto-affectivity. Rather, the 'halo,' as the radical auto-ambiguity of all feeling as such, is *absolutely indifferent* to the fixed (i.e. unambiguous) contours of things like 'self' and 'other.' In much the same manner, Buddhism deproblematizes the phony self-and-other claptrap by beforehand emptying 'self' and 'other' of intrinsic reality. If 'self' is nothing, if 'other' is nothing,' and if therefore also 'world,' 'relations,' and 'love' are nothing – then nothing can prevent feeling from *feeling* the suffering of 'someone' or 'something' precisely as feeling (i.e. suffering) ...and not as the feeling (the suffering) 'of someone,' 'of something.' I am not saying, of course, that 'Weymouth,' as the work's amorous-life nimbus, is 'nothing,' and I am certainly not saying that auto-ambiguity in *Weymouth Sands* is a 'Buddhist' nothing. What I am saying is that the thematization of vivisection, indeed of extreme suffering in general (486-488), is not 'added' to the foregrounding of love-delight and contemplative happiness. It may be that a character, indeed a certain reader, encounters pain as antithesis to deliciousness: but 'Weymouth' cannot *not* know suffering, auto-ambiguity as 'Absolute' cannot *not* know vivisection.

In *Owen Glendower*, vivisection (indeed physical suffering in general) is focussed in a way that does not allow us to see 'it' within the halo of the work's overall auto-ambiguity; for the truth of the matter is that in his later works John Cowper Powys was no longer able to consistently phenomenalize auto-ambiguity as a sense of the *uninterrupted* life of the 'Absolute.' This uninterruptedness, permitting ambiguity to be absolute and permitting the absolute to be ambiguity, is what Magnus Muir becomes aware of as "a strange feeling of some secret continuity in experience that was the only thing that mattered" (496). Vivisection in no way 'interrupts' *Weymouth Sands*, for the kind of mind that implements scientific pain is beforehand visualized as operating within 'Weymouth,' within the ambiguous pleasure-pain continuum of sustained auto-affectivity as such. *Owen Glendower* sports something that we may call 'history' or 'Wales' – but 'history'/ 'Wales' is by no means as powerful, as *luminous*, as 'Weymouth.' *Owen Glendower* does not foreground a dominant sense of affective simultaneity. In *Weymouth Sands*, as in a haze, each unit is the *affective simultaneity* of all the others. "But simultaneously with this impression [of the personality of Dr. Mabon] there rose up in the background of his thoughts all the old landmarks together, the Spire, the Statue, the Nothe, the Bridge" (494). Such an ambiguous simultaneity is affective, affectivity permitting each object to "assert itself...with an interior illumination, as if it were independent both of darkness and light" (493). The "interior illumination" does not belong to external reality (objectivity *qua* objectivity) or to the mind (subjectivity *qua* subjectivity), or indeed to the interaction between these. The "interior illumination" belongs rather to the affective simultaneity as such. This extraordinary luminosity, which is inseparable from the terraqueous halo-feeling, from the seaside town as pearly 'haze,' may be seen in the work's readiness to foreground ambiguous deliciousness at the heart of physical and mental misery. For Ruth Loder the physical suffering of her father is atrocious; yet "what really diffused itself through her mind in spite of many twinges of nerve-to-nerve sympathy was a mysterious, inscrutable sense of satisfaction that she lived where there were greenish-coloured fish and where greenish-coloured fish could *go out on the tide*" (486). The sense of diffusion in the words *go out on the tide*, italicized by John Cowper, has nothing to do with transcendence, if by transcendence we mean a going-out that oversteps some sort of 'here' into some sort of 'other,' 'over there,' or 'beyond.' The sense of going out on the tide has got nothing to do with outerness, with going-out as such. It has to do, rather, with the terraqueous life, with 'Weymouth' as auto-luminous, absolute ambiguity. Ruth "retained all the while a large portion of her consciousness entirely calm, occupied indeed with matters far removed from ...James Loder's ulcers ...What she was thinking about were certain greenish-coloured fish that she had seen that afternoon below Sandsfoot Castle as she took care of Captain Poxwell. They had dark fins, erect and very sharp. She wondered to herself if they were in that pool still or if they had gone out with the tide" (485-486). We see here that in *Weymouth Sands*, 'thinking' is no mere cogitation but auto-affectivity – an affectivity which returns 'to' itself, much as the tide does, in order to confirm the sense not of its certainty but of its self-illuminating ambiguity. To be "thinking about" certain "greenish-coloured" fish and to wonder if they are "in that pool still" or vanished from it "with the tide" is not really to probe into the 'either-or' of possible location ...as if the situatedness of the fish would matter. The ambiguity is not intellectual. Nor is it in fact emotional. The pool and the far-off zones of the tide are not separate sources of emotion. There is no hesitation between the one and the other, so that affectivity could be theorized as a hesitancy-affect. Instead affectivity is nothing other than a sense *that* one is emotively alive. This 'that' is and is not emotive. The 'that' of the sensation *that* I am alive is here itself that which is 'greenish-coloured.'

The "infinite satisfaction" provided by the sensory details of the terraqueous life nourishes "the under-life with which her nature was sub-charged" (486). Such an 'under-life' is the "secret, elemental life" at the forefront of the attention of the typical Powys hero (482). As in a halo, such life is at once substance and not-substance, at once something material-substantial and something 'below' the material-substantial. The under-life is in a manner of speaking "sub-substantial" (472). This strangely-coined word points to a peculiar transcendence which does not transcend, to an odd 'beyond' that is not shot past the horizon, as it were, but *felt* on this side of ordinary, mundane phenomenalization. The 'holiday' aura of Weymouth signals this type of non-transcendent transcendence ...so that *on the sand*s holiday-pleasure is not conceived as a remote possibility or far-fetched dream but as an immanent quality of the most ordinary movements and perceptions. From the perspective of such a transcendence-without-transcendence, or transcendence-on-this-side-of-transcendence, it is easy to see that the perpetually re-defined dividing line between 'wet sand' and 'dry sand' is nothing other than an internalization of a remote, conventional dividing line – the one which, much like the horizon, signals the supposed gap between world and beyond-world. We may consider the 'under-life' of someone like Ruth Loder as a 'sub-substantial' realm in which there is beforehand a *becoming-aquatic* of such an internalization of transcendental borders. Just as the line of demarcation between 'wet sand' and 'dry sand' is slightly more *aquatic* than a traditional, Platonic, sky-oriented line of demarcation between the world and the transcendent, so in Ruth's "private underworld of well-being – full of greenish-coloured fish, floating and drifting, full of sunlit waters, rocking and tossing" (486), the 'sub-substantial' (472) act of hallucinating aqueous life "*below* Sandsfoot Castle" (485; emphasis added) is an act in which the dividing-line between "they were in that pool still" and "they had gone out with the tide" (486) is an *aquatic* dividing-line ...a dividing line that has beforehand become assimilated into the generalized terraqueous affectivity of the work. This sense of the aquatic immanency of limits, which in *Weymouth Sands* is nothing other than the affective ideativity of the self-presence of the artifact, is not in its essence to be confused with amphibiousness. The 'sub-substantial' under-life is not 'able' to live in two zones rather than simply in one. The "underworld of well-being" is not one thing as well as something else. Terraqueous auto-ambiguity is not a function of an amphibious versatility which allows feeling to 'combine' water and earth, pool and horizon. It is rather a matter of a 'humid' surrealism given to 'Weymouth' itself as translucent ambiguity.

The integrity, indeed glory, of feeling depends on the immanent intactness that ensures feeling's *absolute* reception of itself as itself only. Accordingly, the content or 'subject-matter' of feeling is in a sense a matter of indifference. *This indifference, the 'indifference' of pain and pleasure, their radical co-belonging to one and the same mode of phenomenalization, is of course no matter of indifference to the one who feels.* For the one who feels something right now there is a terrible difference between happiness and misery, between pleasure and pain. The one *is* not the other. Nevertheless, feelings are *not* different from each other in terms of their way of appearing to us as that which, indubitably, they are. The indubitability of pain and the indubitability of pleasure are one and the same indubitability, *viz.*, the indubitability of feeling. It is for reasons such as these that, without any loss of æsthetic or affective *vraisemblance*, *Weymouth Sands* can pass *immediately* from the pleasing absoluteness of the "greenish-coloured" under-life of Ruth Loder to the cruel absoluteness of the reddish-coloured under-life of James Loder's ulcers.

In the act of recalling *Weymouth Sands* as imaginative experience, one is not likely to immediately think of the cruel, the gross, the violent, or the revolting. In point of fact, however, there are moments of grotesque physical horror here that equal anything thrown into *Owen Glendower*. The latter *tries* to be grotesque, and deliberately manufactures mediæval Welsh war-life as a chamber of horrors. History is consciously visualized as a tapestry in which horror and romance are intertwined – 'time' being as it were an interval between a unit of evil and a moment of idealized glory, between a moment of idealized glory and its material punctuation. There is thus a progressive 'erosion' of romance in *Owen Glendower*, so that what finally remains of romance is essentially irreal, possibly mere legend and fantasy. This is not so in

Weymouth Sands. Here there is no chiaroscuro of negativity and positivity. It is rather the case that evil in its affective tremor is indifferently also compassion in *its* affective tremor. That which superficially speaking is 'shocking' in *Weymouth Sands* in no way upsets the equanimity of the work's affective optimism. In *Owen Glendower* sadism, masochism, and sado-masochism are deployed over the entire history of nation and over the entire fate of the man of destiny. Experience is a network of scars – each one with its own sordid tale to tell about the quasi-psychotic extravagances of humanity. *Owen Glendower* is in essence a disquisition on mastery and servitude, 'freedom' being a sort of 'time out' enjoyed in the lacunæ of time's inexorable onwardness. No such thing can be said about *Weymouth Sands*. The 'telepathy' of the Weymouth landmarks is no crisscrossing of emotive signals. 'Weymouth' is not semiotic. Nor is it 'historical.' The malice prompting James Loder to appear stark naked before his daughter during his fits of ulcerous pain (486-487) is certainly, *as behaviour*, nothing less than sadism. But the whole point of course is that this sadistic behaviour does not arise in the artifact as behaviour but as affectivity. Affectivity is by no means behaviour. I may behave badly, behave like a good boy, behave like a king, behave like a spoilt child, behave like a god, like an idiot ...but this really tells us nothing about affectivity. Everything depends on the affective context in which behaviour makes its appearance. In reviewing the information that James Loder "had long ago, in fits of pain, inured his daughter to seeing him naked" (486), and in discovering furthermore that on the present occasion Ruth "knew well enough that he had not stripped himself naked, nor had stretched himself out like this, *until they began to ascend the stairs*" (487), we cannot overlook the fact that these units of information are *immediately* preceded by the observation that Ruth "carried her private underworld of well-being – full of greenish-coloured fish, floating and drifting, full of sunlit waters, rocking and tossing – quite *unashamedly* to her father's bedroom" (486; emphasis added). As a consequence of the general sense of the vitality of each and every "underworld of well-being," the acute horror of human-animal suffering is beforehand recognized as having roots in a general auto-affectivity which itself is neither horrible nor zoological. The various zany, 'zoological' incidents in *Weymouth Sands* are thus, unlike their counterparts in *Owen Glendower*, no free-floating islands of emotive energy pointing primarily to themselves but affective landmarks forwarding our overall sense of being progressively initiated into the full range of affects that conjointly make up 'Weymouth' as a terraqueous absolute. The fact that "James Loder actually had the gall, in the midst of his acute suffering, to make a gross reference to the trade of an abortionist" (487) does not come as a shock, any more than does information about the loony domestic rituals of Sylvanus Cobbold. Somehow the ulcers of James Loder ("There's a red circle of them in here!" 487) are no more dangerous to the work's halo of affective ideativity than are the pseudo-religious 'Caput' ...'Anus' rigmaroles of the seaside prophet (483). In an important sense, all real-life negativity is relativized in the way that the wet sand and the dry sand conjointly relativize the heartless antics of Mr. Punch on Weymouth Beach (458). This is not to say that suffering is not *felt* in *Weymouth Sands*. It is to say that even the most acute forms of human-animal suffering are conceived in relation to some 'underlife' of well-being – the superiority of which lies in its ambiguity, its lack of limiting specificity.

When, a moment ago, I called attention to the fact that 'no one' perceived or felt the long procession of small white clouds passing several hours before dawn over the rooftop of the Sea-Serpent's Head, this *missing receptivity* (the 'no one' unable to receive the affectivity of the passing clouds) was understood as the zero-point of affectivity as such – feeling *itself* being something that does not need a go-between between itself and itself to be that which it is. The nullity of such a go-between, the perfect lack of interval between any feeling and itself, *is* the very materiality of feeling. During the phenomenalization of any feeling, I can actually *feel* the lack of any interval between that specific feeling and itself. In fact the lack-of-interval sensation is precisely that which allows feeling to manifest itself *as* feeling in the first place. The indubitability of feeling is the indubitability of the nullity of the interval between phenomenalization and itself. I am saying, then, that when the narrator permits us to *feel* a slowly-passing procession of small white clouds, and when he simultaneously gives us to understand that 'no one' was there to be affected by the truth of such a night-sight, he is surreptitiously implying that despite this nullity of someone-there-to-see-and-feel, or in fact precisely *on account* of this nullity, the cloud-procession is there above pre-dawn Dorchester *as feeling*. Feeling is *there*, as it were, whether there is 'someone' there to feel 'it' or not. The nullity of feeling's middle, the radical superfluity in emotion of any sort of internal go-between, is a 'no-between,' a null-point, a 'no one,' a blank. Now I would like to argue that in *Weymouth Sands* not only long processions of slowly-moving night-clouds but also *pain* is phenomenalized 'around' such a null-point. Put simply, this means that what primarily feels human-animal pain is not an animal or a human but *pain itself*. There is a null-point in pain itself; and during the course of pain taken to the extreme limit of the possible, the suffering animal or suffering person *becomes* this null-point. Such a becoming-null-point of pain is obviously not a becoming-null of pain. Yet it is in a peculiar sense a becoming-null of the animal or human being undergoing pain. Such an understanding of suffering is conveyed to us on numerous occasions also in *Owen Glendower*. As null-point, pain is a peculiar emancipation of life from all personalistic existence. Instead of a human being: pain. Instead of an animal: pain. Instead of a woman: pain. Instead of a man: pain. In a strange way there is a foreshortening of existence in pain. There is pain rather than existence, affectivity rather than consciousness. It is my view that episodes in *Weymouth Sands* and *Owen Glendower* that focus on torture are metaphysically and æsthetically unintelligible without the above-mentioned sense of affectivity as null-point. But let there be no mistake: *Weymouth Sands* does not discuss torture half-heartedly, through mere reference. What is phenomenalized is the human animal on the rack, reduced to a pure nullification of itself. "He [James Loder] was stark naked now. He was stretching himself out on the extreme edge of the bed, so that having no support for his head, or for his buttocks, he might balance himself upon the middle of his spine, as a plank, in the game of see-saw, is balanced on its wooden cross-beam. Mr. Loder, by long and bitter experience, had found out that, when you have ulcers, uncomfortable positions are better than comfortable ones" (486).

In *Weymouth Sands*, affectivity's null-point is a cosmic, ontological null-point. James Loder's hideous pain-discourse is uttered "as if these ulcers of his were in the throbbing midriff of the universe" (488). The null-point is in the midriff of affectivity, and affectivity is in the midriff of life. Accordingly, since affectivity is in the midriff of 'Weymouth,' the *null-point* is in the midriff of 'Weymouth.' As affectivity, such a null-point is in essence Christian rather than Buddhistic, for the null-point is *felt*, not simply acknowledged as nullity. In no way whatsoever does 'Weymouth' forward the overall sensation that life is nothingness. Quite the contrary, life is affectivity. Suffering is real. Far from lacking intrinsic reality, suffering is a rendezvous with the really intrinsic – with affectivity. There is, to be sure, a 'numbness' that goes along with pain. The null-point irradiates a certain 'indifference.' But this 'indifference' does not level down pain (or any other feeling) to a zero-level, to a numb plateau where feeling is no more 'real' than anything else. The specific 'indifference' irradiated by feeling's null-point is instead ultimately one that makes feelings 'indifferent' in relation to *each other*. The null-point of love, the null-point of hate, the null-point of jealousy, the null-point of melancholia, the null-point of fatigue, the null-point of self-confidence are in the final analysis indifferently one and the same null-point, *viz.*, the immanency of feeling as such. All feelings have one thing in common – and this is not simply that they are all 'forms' of feeling but rather that feeling always assumes the same form ...being that which always lacks extension, visibility, dubitability, and internal self-distance. Each significant (or indeed insignificant) character in *Weymouth Sands* has an intuition of this 'indifference.' It is this very 'indifference' in emotion which, on a rarefied level of phenomenalization, 'equalizes' all animal, vegetable, and mineral life. Landmarks too 'feel' the null-point, the equalization – not ultimately because of any animism, telepathy, or supernatural agency, but because of the equalization itself, the absolute lack of inequality between one feeling and another. All feelings are equal, *as feelings*. In a sense not only *Weymouth Sands* but the entire achievement of John Cowper Powys, literary as well as philosophic – is based on this simple but elusive formula.

To slip from one feeling to another, then, is ultimately not merely to 'daydream' but to float through an element – life itself – which, like water, never needs any go-between, interval, or displacement in order to permit a passing-along from one perfectly equalized null-point to another. The equalization is absolute. The passing is absolute. The nullity is absolute. *Feeling* is absolute. 'Weymouth' is nothing other than a name for this absoluteness. To enjoy such affective equalization, to be aware of it and *feel* it as one's "private underworld of well-being" (486), is not merely the Epicurean paradise-sensation of "not to be suffering" (488), but rather a sensation that the Spire, the Nothe, the Statue, the Bridge, and the Monument are one and the same *felt* underlife. In this sense, pain itself may secretly phenomenalize itself as a "private underworld of well-being" – and it is from this perspective that I conceive not only James Loder's exhibitionism but also his actual pain.

•

No reader of *Weymouth Sands* can avoid the impression that suffering such as that of James Loder is somewhat different in its mode of phenomenalization from suffering in animals caused by 'science.' I m not suggesting that human suffering is different in any important way from animal suffering. Nor am I suggesting that ulcerous pain is any more or any less auto-affective than the pain felt by cats and dogs during vivisection. What I *am* saying is that an animal that is hurt in vivisection is not merely subjected to pain; in *addition*, the animal is subjected to a mundanizing of pain. This mundanizing of suffering occurs in and as the transformation of the 'invisibility' of pain (of its null-pointedness as auto-agitation) into representational space. As in the case of bull-fighting, vivisection *stages* suffering. This 'staging' of pain – the act of placing it in an arena where 'it' is presumed to be made visible – can only come about through a failure to recognize pain's nature ...its retreat from the world and its immanent materialization *on this side* of the world, *on this side* of deployment. By definition a feeling cannot have spatial extension – any more than an 'I' or a 'reader' can be a form of extendedness. But during vivisection 'science' superimposes such an illusion. In this way there is added to the animal's suffering not only the arena in which 'observation' can infinitize its appetite for pathological gloating but also the humiliating awareness on the part of suffering that its reality is always secretly in excess of what the world is pretending to visualize, measure, and define. John Cowper's well-known hatred of vivisection is in this way more than a warm-hearted defence of the harmless victims of cynical experimentation. His hatred of 'scientific' pain is part and parcel of his philosophic outlook – part and parcel of an *affective materialism* which is utterly incompatible with the idea that pain could be 'scientific.' 'Science' in this cynical and brutal sense is that which does not have access to the materiality of life – this materiality being in the final analysis nothing other than the immanent tangibility of feeling as such.

The pain of a human being like James Loder is in essence compatible with an 'underlife' of well-being. The pain of a dog subjected to vivisection is not. When the narrator speaks of a future "after Science has killed God, tortured the last animal to death, suckled all babies with machines, eavesdropped on the privacy of all souls, and made life to its last drop an itch of the blood" (472), any reader familiar with the non-fictional, philosophic works of John Cowper knows that such a polarization of 'Science' and 'underlife' ("the privacy of all souls") is by no means a mere viewpoint of fiction but part and parcel of the Cowperist outlook in general. Although it is sloppy to fail to make a distinction between fiction by Powys and philosophy by Powys, there can be little doubt that John Cowper is himself involved, as it were, in the generalized concern about a cynically rationalized planetary life in which "Science did create a fresh race of Sippy-Cattistocks" (472). But as we all know, 'God' is also used in a quite different sense throughout the works of Powys. On the one hand 'God' is the affective 'underlife,' auto-affectivity as the 'Absolute'; on the other hand, 'God' is the very opposite of this 'underlife' – the power that *permits* suffering, including the suffering of vivisected dogs in Hell's Museum. Annabel, the Spy Croft parlour-maid, is sickened by all the exaggerated talk about the *mental* suffering of Captain Poxwell - and in calling attention to the quality of pain endured by James Loder when she has seen him "'thrust his knuckles into the pit of his stomach'" and "'twist on floor, like a waspy what a kitten have caught,'" she speaks of "'what the dear Lord allows us to suffer'" (422-423). This commentary is paradigmatic. On countless occasions, the novels of John Cowper Powys stage the event in which a human being 'defies' the godhead by 'accusing' the Absolute of letting pain happen. It is on occasions such as these that Powys can be seen to be a Christian writer rather than a Stoic philosopher - for the transition from the Stoic world of antiquity to the modern world of Christian affectivity is essentially a transition where the foundation of life is not the refusal of pain but its acknowledgement, not the overcoming of affectivity but its *absolute* recognition. In this sense, Christianity is in a strange way a refutation of the godhead - a transition, if you like, from 'God' to Christ. Such a transition has to do with a sense of the sheer materiality of pain. However, this materiality has no extension. It cannot be seen or represented. It can only be felt. The pre-eminence of John Cowper Powys is not that he is somehow superior in the writerly ability to 'represent' affectivity. Quite the contrary. If this writer has any superiority of genius over his fellow-artists, it lies in his ability to let affectivity be *felt*. The letting-be-felt of affectivity, including the letting-be-felt of the affective act of eschewing undesirable affectivity, needs to be understood and critically described. Otherwise one is not describing the writer's achievement but only a convenient representation of it. The letting-be-felt of affectivity ...this is precisely 'Christianity.' The letting-be-felt of Christianity itself has very little to do with church dogma. It has to do with the way in which one is open to the phenomenalization of feeling in feeling itself - with the way in which one is open to the absoluteness (pure indubitability) of this arising. It is ultimately this indubitability which is disregarded in our times, not only by 'science' in Hell's Museum but by 'science' in Hell's Criticism - in that criticism which asks us to believe that our feelings are not real, that there is some interval, difference, or phenomenological distance between a feeling and itself, between the reality of the affective life and the consciousness of that reality.

When we are told that James Loder's "atheist son...gloated over his pain," and when we are subsequently informed by Annabel that this selfsame pain is "what the dear Lord allows us to suffer" (422-423), 'atheism' and 'the Lord' are curiously implied in each other. The 'Lord' typically rejected by the Powys-narrator is thus a sort of master-God who is unmovingly detached in Stoic fashion from his own affective body, from Creation. Such a 'Lord' is lord over affectivity and is not identical with affectivity as such. In contrast, 'Christ' refuses such detachment, and refuses it precisely as body, as flesh, as matter, as suffering and affectivity. By not being external to affectivity, *but its ongoing manifestation and manifestedness*, 'Christ' personifies affectivity as auto-affection, as feeling letting-itself-be-felt as itself. John Cowper's elegant management of this issue is in no place shown more clearly than in the ability to point to the ongoing auto-phenomenalization of feeling in those very beings who found, or think they found, their lives on a heathen, forward-driving formula of willed 'overcoming.' Dog Cattistock, belonging as he does to a classicist blood-and-iron ideology, is not cut off entirely from the narrator's sympathy for the simple reason that Cattistock cannot escape from the auto-incarnation his businesslike life-attitude obsessively tries to nullify. After stating that the scientific affectivity of Dr. Bush is the sense of the pleasure of "pursuing the horrible truth created by God" (439), the narrator moves on to "what Cattistock felt" (439) prior to the exhibitionist act of swimming out to a cask floating in the stormy sea. He thought of the perfect smoothness of Hortensia Lily's satiny legs "as he had hoped not only to feel them in bed but to see them exposed for his pleasure when she rose in the morning" (440). But the idea that he thinks of this waiting woman "breathing hard with excitement" between white sheets is far less interesting than the idea that his "will to mastery" is no mere cognitive entity or even "body consciousness" but "something in his being" which makes its appearance "like an emanation" (440). In point of fact we are led to believe that those whose programmatic life-attitude is a total disregard for the 'underlife' of well-being are ultimately swayed by that very 'underlife.' Cattistock's reckless decision to plunge into the ocean does not really come exclusively from his brain but from the affective "consciousness" of his "body," "from its mysterious diffused life" (440). This "underlying consciousness" is "not limited to his skull"; nor is it a "spiritual entity" (440). As "body consciousness" (440) this affective ideativity is "a certain mysterious, unknown life-tract" (442). 'Amorous life' may be understood in a man and a woman as a shared sensation that this, the mysteriously unknown life-tract, is what both "wanted" (440).

•

Vivisection-pain is detestable and ugly because it is not co-extensive with any sense of an 'underlife' of well-being. It is that pain and that event which threatens such an 'underlife.' For how could anyone really live in the to-and-fro of the tides of well-being, if somewhere nearby, in the immediate outskirts of one's personal existence, 'experiments' are conducted by individuals who concern themselves no more with the material essences of a mysterious life-tract than with the material essences of flying saucers or with the material essences of little green men from Mars? To vivisect a dog is by the same token to vivisect the materiality of the unknown life-tract, to annul the affective reality of the 'underlife' as viable and possible ground for subsisting happiness. Nevertheless, Hell's Museum is not strong enough to hurt the generalized sense of 'underlife' in *Weymouth Sands*. There are times, such as the sections conjointly dominated by Bush and Cattistock (433-442), when the novel seems to be heading for the kind of disenchanted, de-energized prose to be found in parts of *Owen Glendower*. There are times when this post-coital, self-neutralized pathos may give the superficial reader the impression that the discourse of simple folks (421-427), emerging as it does from a generalized sense of tragic affectivity, is going to lead, as in Hardy, to an overall sense of modern disillusion. But in point of fact the buoyancy of uneducated souls in *Weymouth Sands* is not muted by a sense of their being the playthings of a weary and disillusioned narrator-God. On the contrary, and following the guidelines of Dickens rather than of Hardy, the simple sense of disappointment is itself a source of profound life-enjoyment (427). When Gipsy May wickedly cuts off Sylvanus Cobbold's moustaches, this moustache-vanishing is obviously a life-illusion-vanishing (405-406). But the work itself is not truncated in its generalized affectivty by this loss of life-illusion. Happiness itself never loses its moustaches in *Weymouth Sands*. There is no lessening of 'Weymouth' in the sense that there is in *Owen Glendower* a lessening of 'Wales.' 'Wales' goes underground in order to survive. (And there is, to be sure, a sense of possible resurrection, or at least of political-national renewal.) But 'Weymouth' cannot be thought of as 'going underground,' as becoming an 'underground' movement. The 'underlife' is not an underground movement – for it is not a 'movement' in the first place ...but life as such, its material essence. 'Glyn Dwr' as mythology has to *fail* in order to shimmer. 'Wales' has to retreat. Magnus Muir needs to 'retreat' in order to *be* fully in the 'underlife' of the mysterious, unknown life-tract; but since, without any retreating whatever, even an extrovert person like Dog Cattistock comes to know the 'underlife' of the mysteriously unknown life-tract, we cannot say that retreat is the condition of possibility for 'Weymouth.' Rather, 'Weymouth' is a generalized retreat beforehand, whether one 'retreats' or not. Magnus may lose Curly, Sylvanus may lose his moustaches – but 'Weymouth' cannot lose the 'Absolute,' and the 'Absolute' itself cannot lose the 'Absolute.' (Sylvanus in fact *goes on* addressing the 'Absolute' after the loss of his moustaches.) The 'Absolute,' in other words auto-affectivity, cannot itself become disillusioned – for in an important sense it is not in time, not subject to change, not subject to the doings of man, whether 'scientific' or historiographic. Affectivity itself cannot 'become disillusioned.' It simply affects itself. In this sense, and utterly in opposition to everything promulgated by Hardy, 'amorous life' is not affected by hazard – not even when hazard ruins all. For the 'amorous life' is ultimately that which remains when all is lost, as the condition of possibility *for* loss and *for* that which was lost. 'Amorous life' as auto-ambiguity cannot 'be disappointed' ...any more than a cloud can 'be disappointed.' Beings can be "crestfallen" (423). But being itself, which in *Weymouth Sands* is *well*-being, cannot be crestfallen. No well-being, *as* well-being, has ever been 'crestfallen.' No 'underlife' can take a tumble. It is not 'up' somewhere in the first place. The 'underlife' of well-being cannot be divided by an interval separating 'low' from 'high,' any more than such a hypothetical interval could slice the 'underlife' into a 'here' and a 'there.' Like the sea, the 'underlife' is already down under. But this 'down under' indicates no position. 'Down under' is much like '*on this side* of.' It is an arch-position pointing to the erasure of positionality.

From this type of archi-perspective, or non-perspective, one may readily see that the event of deferral and prolongation – as during the work's inaugural disquisitions on the delay of Perdita's ferry – far from marking the introjection in affectivity of the interval, marks affectivity itself, the perpetual lingering of Magnus Muir in Magnus Muir; the perpetual lingering of Weymouth in 'Weymouth,' the perpetual lingering of the 'underlife' in itself. What lingers, *without interval*, in waiting is waiting. Even in the most impatient and frustrated waiting there is an element of well-being and abiding – a sense of the perpetuity of life. As boredom, this sense of perpetuity beclouds the souls of many a melancholy figure in Weymouth. But this very melancholia occurs within a lack of distance diffused by the sound, sight, and generalized idea of the sea. This sea, by rolling over itself, diffuses an emanation which in this work is recognized as an element that is indistinguishable from affectivity as such. In the receiving of our boredom there is thus a reception also of that which makes boredom possible in the first place – and this originary 'extra,' as a null-point of all affective life, is in *Weymouth Sands* a mysterious tonic, one that translates the harsh, powerful cries of the gulls themselves into something that is not itself harsh or powerful, the nervousness of the "[n]ervous mothers" into a generalized nervous excitement that is not itself strictly nervous or agitated (456).

The 'Absolute' is not seized "in vacuo" (402), for the 'underlife' of well-being is not itself phenomenalized "in vacuo." "[T]he Absolute was to be found in the concrete and not in the abstract" (402). The null-point of all feeling, the 'invisible' midriff where it rolls over itself to be that which it is, *namely feeling*, does not phenomenalize itself in or as nothingness. If the null-point were nothingness, it could not be felt. If the null-point, say, of jealousy were 'nothing,' then the feeling 'jealousy' would be the feeling of nothing, not the feeling 'jealousy.' I write the feeling 'jealousy' rather than *the feeling 'of' jealousy* – for the idea of 'of' is just as mistaken as the idea of 'nothing.' 'Jealousy' is a feeling, and certainly not a feeling 'of' this or that. We might say, then, that although the null-point of each and every feeling is not 'nothing,' it is not 'something' either; it is not a visible 'X' or a visible 'Y'; it is not the go-between 'A' or the go-between 'B'. (The expression "a feeling 'of' jealousy" creates the impression that 'of' is a go-between.) Now it is my view that in *Weymouth Sands* everything depends in the final analysis on the sense of the 'underlife' of well-being as something that, without actually hesitating or equivocating, hovers mid-way between an invisible-visible 'nothing' and a visible-invisible 'something.' As I have suggested earlier, the idea or image of a *pearly* nebulousness catches this sense of the almost-nothing or almost-something at the heart of auto-affectivity as 'underlife.' If the sea is a "pearl-soft sea" (336), if hazy sunshine is "pearl-soft sunshine" (338), and if the name of someone called "Pearl Water" enables the narrator to inform us that Magnus recalls "Pearl talking to him once" (372), we are entitled to read units of information like "Pearl died" (373) as units situated within a generalized sense of life as 'underlife,' of 'underlife' as well-being, and of well-being as being "transported...to the magic shore of some halcyon sea" (456). The fact that the pearliness of this sea is adjacent to something utterly non-pearly, *viz.*, the gross, repulsive, and disgusting (382), does not prevent, endanger, or even diminish the diffusion of the pearl-feeling as atmospherium of horizon, water, and air. Units of 'Rabelaisian' grossness or naked definition may "emerge from a pleasant nebulosity into a biting clarity" (402), but the pearly nebulosity always returns – like the meteorological phenomenon of sea-hazes as such. On a particular afternoon, a certain "diffused sunlight" may be so "filmy" that an "ideal atmosphere" is formed – one that is so fresh and pearly that it "resembled the air of Watteau's 'Embarkation to Cytherea'" (456). The feeling in

Weymouth Sands that such an "ideal atmosphere" is the aboriginary atmospherium of the entire work cannot simply be written off by means of a rationalist psychology encouraging us to understand vision as the nostalgic idealizations of an infantilized hero seeing 'reality' through the essentializing recollections of "an eternal classical childhood," a "divine limbo of unassailable play-time" (457). The Cytherea-quality, far from being confined to the originating childhoods of character or narrator, inheres in quite other childhoods, *viz.*, those of feelings themselves. It is in the childhood of feeling itself, in feeling's own perpetual newness, that life is pearly. And *this* filmy transparency – of feeling in general and as such – is the *reality* of the 'underlife' – the 'underlife's pearly sensation that it is itself the indubitable. In this pearly newness of all affectivity, well-being and phenomena are one and the same ambiguous life.

Now in the painting *Embarkation to Cytherea* what is painted is not an embarkation – for what Watteau has given us is not a 'what' in the first place ...but a feeling. This feeling, far from pointing to an interval, to some gap between presence and destination, points to itself. The Cytherea-feeling is an 'air.' This air, *qua* air, *qua* affectivity, far from suggesting an instant in which a ship is opening some phenomenological distance between the present and the transcendent ...points to no 'beyond' whatsoever. For the present, the 'air,' beforehand *is* this 'beyond.' This pre-inclusion of the 'beyond' in the present is the quality of the pearl: *in it* transcendency has beforehand happened ...so that one can, as it were, 'see' the foreshortening of distance 'in' the pearlescence. Pearlescence points to the nature of the possibility of transcendence-within-immanence, to feeling in the material state of its most essential condensation. Like the *disembarkation* contemplated by Magnus Muir on the occasion of the arrival of Perdita Wane with the Cherbourg steamer (25), the *embarkation* to Cytherea does not foreground the affectivity of going or the affectivity of arriving but auto-affection as absolute: "On this occasion that sudden whistle of the Cherbourg steamer produced a very queer impression on his mind. It was an impression as if the whole of Weymouth had suddenly become an insubstantial vapour suspended in space" (25). It is naive to believe that such words primarily refer to a fictive subjectivity which, in stimulus-response manner, is sent from 'external' sensations to 'internal' ones. The literary achievement, here, is neither the one of representing human behaviour, nor the one of representing consciousness. The aim is to adumbrate affectivity as 'underlife.' This aim is already taken by the fact that the affectivity of 'disembarkation' surreptitiously foreshadows the ideativity of the 'embarkation to Cytherea.'

The 'underlife' of well-being recognizes "the pleasure which there is in life itself" (406). This pleasure is in an important sense real only *on this side* of the world. The 'underlife' is not really *there* in the world, or in the mind for that matter. Accordingly the vanishing of Sylvanus's great moustaches, the feeling that suddenly "there was nothing *there*!" (408; emphasis added), is in the final analysis just as unimportant as the failure of Magnus Muir to be quite *'all there.'* For Mrs Wix, the idea that her daughter is being courted by someone who is "not quite *'all there'*" (314, 315) simply means that Magnus is somewhat mentally inadequate; but the general sensation throughout *Weymouth Sands* is that this tendency of the 'underlife' not to be there (not to be in the world) is a token of sanity. The ultimate health is "the sanity of Not-Being" (452). This Not-Being is an etherealization of the world – but this etherealization, because it appears materially as the materiality of feeling, is *concrete phenomenon*. Such is indeed the astonishment of Watteau's *Embarkation to Cytherea*. Beauty, in other words the material painting itself, that which our 'underlife' *actually touches*, is not ideal but real, not abstract but concrete, not theorized but affectively thought ...thought affectively in that realm of 'pearly' condensation where ideativity itself is concrete, is *my* thought, *this* life, *this* embarkation. Not-to-be-all-there ...this is a condition of possibility for the embarkation to Cytherea. But this condition does not merely stay away at some far-off horizon, as a mere hypothesis. Not-being-all-there beforehand materializes; and this *a priori* materialization, the phenomenon of beauty, is the life of the 'underlife,' the pleasure which there is in life itself.

I think that the crowning achievement of *Weymouth Sands* is the work's attempt to understand beauty as the *material presence* of not-being-all-there. In any lesser work, indeed in any lesser writer, the not-being-all-there of the 'underlife' would have been understood as a form of absence or semi-absence. Here the *material presence* of not-being-all-there is religious. That presence *qua* materiality could be not-being-all-there; that not-being-all-there *qua* not-being-all-there could be material presence ...this is strange and immense. The material *absoluteness* of not-being-all-there is the secret of the *Embarkation for Cytherea*. Watteau does not 'depict' something; instead something is materially felt to be absolutely present; and this thing that is felt to be absolutely present, feeling itself as affective matter, is felt in the nullity-transparency of *its presence*. The featherweight sensation in the *Embarkation to Cytherea* is derived from the pure absence of interval between the pleasure there is in life and this life itself as auto-affective nullity. The 'embarkation' that is to happen always already *has* happened ...but this 'has' is in the material present, is presence itself. In *Weymouth Sands*, as in the painting by Watteau, this presence of the not-being-all-there of the 'underlife' is phenomenalized as "beauty itself" (371). 'Beauty' here is no quality or appendage. In a sense it is not even something 'felt.' Curly's beauty is scarcely phenomenal. Curly is "not half as aware of her own beauty as most girls are" (370). She does not really 'feel' her own beauty. So when the narrator informs us that "[s]he *felt* rather than realized how unsatisfied was her claim upon life, her claim upon happiness" (371), we are made to understand that this feeling is not the feeling 'of' someone called Curly 'about' the relationship between her life and her looks.

> Not Curly's intelligence, but, as it were, *her beauty itself,* beyond the margin of her reason, began to make its demands ...It was as if the soft petals of some ill-placed plant should protest, while its root and stalk made no sign, against the sterile spot in which fate had opened them to the air. Her incomparable form and face ...seemed themselves to protest that they deserved something better ...These dumb protests from the transparency of Curly's skin, from the lovely wistfulness of her far-off gaze, from the delicate curves of her slender body, were uttered in voices much more poignant ...than the abrupt and rather contrary sounds emitted by her young lips (371).

Curly does not 'feel' her own beauty, *for this beauty is itself already feeling*, already itself beauty feeling beauty, feeling *feeling* feeling, beauty affecting itself, self-affection without ego. This ipseity without solipsism is visible-invisible in and as Curly's skin. The almost-not-being-there of perfection is the skin-thin almost-nothing of 'beauty itself,' the unidealized (because materially manifest) embarkation of the gaze. Manifestation's "soft petals" are not nourished by any root or stalk – but by themselves. The "voices" (371) of beauty – of skin, gaze, and body-curves – are superior to the "sounds" of language (371). This is not so because beauty is idealized and because Curly's language remains trite, uneducated, pedestrian, and unexalted. The 'voices,' not belonging to any phonic order (to any spectrum of reverberations distanced from each other in musical intervals) are superior because skin, gaze, and body-curves fail altogether to enter the world as reverberation. Curly's physical presence does not articulate itself in a world, or indeed in an idealized world. Magnus Muir is not idealizing Curly. He is seeing her. He is materially feeling her presence, feeling her as presence. This presence is auto-æsthetic rather than æsthetic. The skin, gaze, and body-curves are not strictly speaking *there* at all. They do not belong to an exterior or interior order – but to that which beforehand withdraws from both of these ...the 'underlife.' The presence of the skin, gaze, and body-curves depends on *Curly* – on Curly *rather* than on world or overworld. The vacuity of this double non-depending pre-affects Curly. Her feelings are sensed to be "moving in that region of a girl's being where her whole nature is stirred up" (370). Here specific affects "are only vaguely articulate" (370). But the fact that specific emotions are only vague, or that her overall sense of world-situatedness is only "dim" (370), does not make "her beauty itself" into something vague or dim (371). Her "loveliness" (370) is the loveliness of manifestation as such. That manifestation as such (whatever its 'contents') is an absolute – this is the tale told in *Weymouth Sands*. Accordingly, manifestation has the upper hand over everything: over morality, over personalistic interactivity, over self-interest, and in a sense even over truth. The idea of Curly as a source of designing infidelity "fled away abashed" (370). This shame-faced flight is not triggered by the sense in a middle-aged egoist that her magnificent beauty freely overflows the narrow considerations of adult egotism. It is rather the case that 'loveliness,' by not-being-all-there (in the world) – but only in 'loveliness' – has beforehand put an end to everything that is not affective, not faultless. That which is absolute is not that which is ideal but that which, without setting up any internal space for self-reverberation, is the manifestation of itself only. Ultimately one is given the sense that what manifestation manifests is manifestation only. 'Loveliness' is from this viewpoint not an attribute, thing, or event. Curly may need all kinds of things (flowers, new shoes, a new dress, a new man) ...but her lovelines does not.

It is always a vulgar mistake to interpret such a state of affairs as supposed 'solipsism,' supposed 'autonomy,' or supposed 'self-identity.' In order to eschew this commonplace perspective, *Weymouth Sands* perpetually turns its regard towards phenomena that phenomenalize themselves as pure units of immanent auto-affection. These units typically display an airy-invisible nullity ensuring our reception of them as something other than a reception of a being with an internally reverberating echo. Auto-affection does not take the form of the internal 'pattern' of its own subjective echo. It is itself *without* such an echo, *without* an inwardly opened-up space. Sitting in a pleasure boat, Magnus Muir finds himself immersed in auto-affection.

> And then an odd thing happened to him. He caught sight of a large, derelict piece of cork, the sort of piece of cork that fishermen use to keep their deep sea nets from sinking out of sight. This large piece of cork lay half-embedded in the sand. But no sooner had he caught sight of it than a rush of happiness, so intense, so overwhelming, took possession of him, that he was as one transported out of himself. (478)

The ensuing commentary rationalizes this event by diverting our attention from the immanent phenomenon of the cork to the transcendent childhood experiences of a boy walking with his father to Redcliff Bay. However, the "rush of happiness" does not primarily point to Penn House, Redcliff Bay, or Preston Brook. Rather; the "rush of happiness" points *to the cork*. The past does not all by itself, without any prompting, become a "rush of happiness." The auto-affective or auto-affect*ing* object is typically understood in Powys as a nullity which, in the very null-pointedness of its own equilibrium, points to itself only. The rush of happiness is in the final analysis indistinguishable from *the cork*. "But no sooner had he caught sight of it than a rush of happiness..." (478). The sighting of the cork is ultimately nothing other than the sighting of affectivity by itself – nothing other than the rush in which affectivity immanently knows affectivity ...purely, absolutely, perfectly. The ability of the cork not to transcend itself, not to overstep its own limits, is paradoxically secured by the semblance of transcendence (childhood as far-distant 'beyond'). The thought of childhood may certainly trigger the sensation of happiness, but hardly this special rush of happiness. The rush itself, *qua* rush, is emphatically cork-oriented, not childhood-oriented. "*That piece of cork* became all the summer afternoons when ...*That piece of cork* became the splash of waves into all the..." (478; emphasis added). The generalized feeling produced by these lines is not the banal sensation that there is some trivial link between a character's present consciousness and a character's past consciousness. There is here a feeling that the immanency of 'cork' (its interior, affective, spaceless rush into itself) and the immanency of childhood ("the splash of waves into all the rock-pools," 478) are *one and the same immanency*. 'One and the same' here does not mean 'identity.' The cork is a onefold. Childhood is a onefold. But the absolute perfection of each of these in its inward tightness is not an outcome of the fact that in each case selfsameness prevails over difference. For the type of 'sameness' that governs 'cork' and 'childhood' is perfectly indifferent to 'difference' as well as to 'sameness.' In short, an auto-affective onefold is not rational-conceptual. (Nor is it 'sub-rational,' 'superrational.') The interior 'rush' of the cork (and I am talking about the cork, not about the sight of the cork), the interior 'rush' of childhood – these two rushes rush into each other beforehand ...and the 'underlife' of well-being, without any effort whatever, recognizes itself immediately as this *pure* manifestation of feeling in and as itself.

I am possibly saying, then, that in Powys 'ecstasy' (in the strict sense of a going-out-beyond, in the strict sense of 'transcendence') is no such thing at all – but rather a swoon in which a onefold is permitted to appear purely in the interior rush of immanent life. There is a wonderful sense of this in a passage where 'oolite' and 'balloon' are freely embedded in a double onefold – the 'oo' of 'oolite' and the 'oo' of 'balloon' being the reduplicated ipseity of an interior rush of the world into its own ideative embarkation.

> As Magnus glanced down at this book [Hardy's *Well-Beloved*] he caught the word 'oolite,' and the word seemed to dance before him. A baby, somewhere on their crowded seat ...was holding by a string a rose-coloured toy balloon ...It was upon this rosy toy that the word 'oolite' now fixed itself, like a label on the surface of a red moon, and although the Jobber's stony island was hidden from their eyes at that spot by Weymouth Pier, the tutor had the sensation that the whole of Portland, with all its people and all their passions, was no more solid than this airy, floating ephemeral balloon. (473)

One immanency 'refers' to another. But the 'reference' of the one to the other does not occur in the transcendent area between them, does not occur *in the world,* but rather 'in' the indubitable rush of each self-affecting onefold as it affects itself, *in so far* as it affects itself. The rotundity of 'oolite,' rushing internally through 'oo,' the rotundity of 'balloon,' rushing internally through 'oo,' are not *felt* to be 'two' rotundities belatedly setting up some 'rapport' in referential space. Reference is not due to referentiality, the possibility of reference, but due to the lack of this possibility. The not-being-balloon of oolite, the not-being-oolite of balloon, are the vacuity that leaves something absolutely open – the wide-open nihil in which a tutor of classical languages discovers that "the whole of Portland" is a stony island floating in air. Freedom, here, is the vanishing of all the poly-semiotic haberdashery of discursive reality – the sense in each aristocratic or unaristocratic tramp on this planet that in the underlife's interior rush our well-being knows a solidity without interval or space ...a solidity which is just as indubitable in a balloon or in a dream as it is in "the whole of Portland." Nothing is more solid than "a rose-coloured toy balloon." Nothing is farther away from space, from self, and from the world. That "the whole of Portland" is "no more solid" than the balloon (473) does not mean that the balloon is not solid, *that air is not solid.* It means that the stone island and the balloon are co-solid. Air is as solid as stone. Stone is as solid as air. Air and stone are no longer elements but sub-elemental units *of affectivity.* The affectivity of stone and the affectivity of air are one and the same affectivity, *viz.*, affectivity as such. As affectivity, as 'underlife,' air and stone are not simply on a par but absolutely on a par. 'Stone' emerges out of this parity. So does air. 'Stone' *phenomenalizes* itself out of this parity, like air. 'Air' *appears* in and as this parity – as does stone. Consequently, the generalized sense in *Weymouth Sands* that solid, monumental entities effortlessly 'speak' to each other is not at all brought over to us as a sense that there is first a distribution of solid landmarks, and then only subsequently some supposedly semiotic interactivity 'between' them. There is in fact no foregrounded sense of semiosis whatsoever. It is rather the case that, on account of the pre-arranged *affective parity* of air, stone, and water, that which is stone is by the same token air, just as that which is air by the same token is stone. As affectivity, the Spire, the Nothe, the Statue, or the Monument does not have to 'step out' into air in order to 'pass on' something like a 'communication.' Such stepping-out (transcendence) is superfluous in a field of underlife or underlives where no transcendent milieu (no world) is actualized in the first place. 'Weymouth' is not a world. It is a field of immanency where the interval (all sense of intervening difference, of semiotic hiatus) is reduced and refined to something as paradigmatic and elusive as the *non-lineal* (pre-mundane, pre-Cartesian, pre-geometric) line of demarcation between 'wet sand' and 'dry sand.' The extraordinary and 'absolute' pre-eminence of this wet-dry affectivity is not organized around the commonsensical intuition of the mutual exclusiveness of 'wet' and 'dry' but rather around the reverse of this ...the sense that 'wet' and 'dry' are affective equals, both of them being in the final analysis 'sand.' The wet-sand-and-dry-sand-affectivity has for its condition of possibility the affective parity of air, stone, and water.

    The Powys hero's programmatic determination to "enjoy my sensations" (414) may in the final analysis be understood not as a resistance to the agitations of existence but as a resistance to 'the world' as something setting up an interval (a space) between the interior rush of the affective onefold and itself. To "enjoy my own sensation" is a *thematization* of the ipseity of the inward rush of the affective onefold across its own lack of internal interval. To thematize something is to bring it to the level of self-consciousness, to make it willed, programmatic, ideological, philosophic. But the onefold itself is not philosophic. The rose-coloured red balloon (473) is no more philosophic, as originary auto-affection, than the green parasol "intently" stared-at by Sylvanus Cobbold after the rape of his moustaches (414). It is therefore a mistake to view the hyletic onefold of the affective auto-impression as a 'rush' produced by intentionality. To stare "so fixedly and so intently and so long at the green parasol" is not to *intend* that green parasol – for the green parasol is in the final analysis neither a world-object nor a mind-object but an absolute. This absolute, as spaceless rush of green feeling into green feeling, is an 'opposite' ("at the green parasol *opposite* him") – but 'opposite' here no longer suggests an interval between object-in-the-world and impression-in-mind, for the subjectivity needed to perform such a spacing-out of mind from world is not there in the first place. "He had stared so fixedly and so intently and so long at the green parasol opposite him before he reached his conclusion [to take the loss of his moustaches as 'fate'] that he felt bewildered and confused when he *came to himself*" (414; emphasis added). Sylvanus 'comes' to himself after the intent fixation of the green parasol as 'opposite.' It follows from this that Sylvanus was not strictly speaking *there* (as subjectivity 'opposing' parasol) during the event of gazing "intently." The parasol, as opposite, is really no opposite but a para-opposite, an empty opposite, an other void of alterity ...or if you like an alterity devoid of world, of that sense of Euclidian extendedness in which, exclusively, the alterior can be other. (The fantasy that the moustaches will "grow again, in my coffin" belongs to this realm where phenomenalization, as the growing of appearances into phenomenality, does not occur in the world but *on this side* of it.) One is not surprised to learn that the interval between parasol and mind ("vivid reflection," 416) is invalid once the hallucinated onefold ("interior mechanism," 416) is fully recognized as onefold and not as mind-world interactivity. The idea that the green parasol 'itself' thinks is nothing other than recognition of the fact that the interval separating subjectivity and objectivity is as void of ultimate truth as was the aforementioned interval separating stone and air. "There must have been something *in the interior mechanism* of that green parasol which had a power of vivid reflection" (416; emphasis added). As affectivity, hence as the 'Absolute,' parasol and reflection are on a par – as are the 'Absolute' and the reception of the 'Absolute' (in this case Sylvanus). But to say that 'Sylvanus' is the reception of the 'Absolute' is no more true than to say that the *green parasol* is the reception of the 'Absolute.' And to say that the green parasol is the reception of the 'Absolute' is much like saying that a green 'Absolute' receives itself, and that the perfectedness of the rush of this inwardness, that the perfectedness of the inwardness of this rush ...is the 'Absolute.' Although John Cowper spends quite a lot of time ridiculing not only Sylvanus but also the 'Absolute,' the sensitive reader will be unlikely to make the mistake of failing to intuit the delicate earnestness behind or beneath such irony. Auto-affection, 'Weymouth,' *is the Absolute* – not because of the presumed greatness of a place, not because of the worship of a place, not because of the emotion for a place, but because of the greatness of feeling as such. The "violent struggles" made by a person "to close the green parasol" (416) are almost like futile attempts on the part of the world to deny the indubitabilty of the 'Absolute' – in this case hallucination as the auto-receptivity of a green intentiveness. Sylvanus's "dialogue with his Absolute" (412) is nothing but a dialogue of Sylvanus with himself; but this dialogue of Sylvanus with himself is in its turn a dialogue of the 'Absolute' with *itself.* "'Everything,' the Absolute continued, as his clean-shaven devotee stared at the green parasol with which the elderly gentleman in front of him was using to protect himself from the sun. 'Everything has always changed, and always will. Outside Me, who am Everything, there is Nothing'" (412). Sylvanus has briefly managed "to become for the nonce the Absolute arguing with the Absolute" (412). Sylvanus is aware of the potential solipsism and egotism in such a life-conception ("'I was always *myself with my big moustaches!* ...always they were Me! ...Me and my moustaches,'" 413); but he is also aware of a higher-order conception of this sense of affective onefold, one that precisely is an emancipation *from* solipsism and *from* egotism. (The parasol-ideativity is posterior to the loss of the moustaches and of the life-illusion they symbolize.) "'Are you the First Cause, or are you not?' he kept asking this evasive Entity. And it seemed to him that the Absolute, like that Nothingness which must have confronted Mr. Looney before he drowned himself, replied that It was not the First Cause, or the Last Cause, or any other Cause!" (412). The implication on the larger horizon of the work's affective ideativity is that the 'underlife' of well-being operating throughout *Weymouth Sands* as the quasi-religious backdrop of all truthful reality, while infinitely capable of receiving itself, cannot cause itself. It *is* self-caused, but it *does* not itself cause that which it is. There is in this sense a lack of volition in the green parasol as well as in the 'Absolute,' a lack of volition in 'wet sand' as well as 'dry sand,' in stone as well as sky, in Magnus Muir as well as Sylvanus Cobbold, in the 'loveliness' of Curly Wix as well as in the placid rock-pools recalled by ladies and gentlemen long after the vanishing of the delights of childhood.

•

It is naive to assume that John Cowper would have been reluctant to follow the 'theoretical' remarks in the current reading of *Weymouth Sands*. Indeed there is much evidence in the text to the contrary. The writer is by inclination self-analytical in matters of psychology, philosophy, and ontology. His ongoing analysis of the nature of phenomenalization, far from being amateurish or unsystematic, is shrewd, rigorous, flexible, pointed, and comprehensive. I have already called attention to the fact that the characters who are at the farthest remove from an understanding of life as affectivity nevertheless live, think, and move within life as an affective field – for the simple reason that, as a condition of possibility for all life, affectivity is *ultimately* no less prominent in a hard-headed businessman like Cattistock or in a hard-headed scientist like Bush than it is in characters who are by temperament closer to the writer. A *tour-de-force* in this context is the decision in *Weymouth Sands* to let Dr. Bush be the only character who manages to arrive at something like the work's own conception of the nature of phenomenalization. "[T]here slowly dawned upon Daniel Bush a totally new perspective in scientific psychology" (505). Although his patient, Sylvanus Cobbold, has the upper hand over him, being more "theory-shattering" through the sheer event of living in the very element that the latter only can study and observe, the scientist is nevertheless depicted as one who is on the right track. What is new about the theory-shattering discoveries of Dr. Bush is that he has disconnected himself from the traditional conception of phenomenalization. Phenomena are now no longer regarded as appearances concealing a realm of unconscious or unknowable reality. Phenomena do not point to an Unconscious, to a dark region that is transcendent to ongoing phenomenalization as such. "The breaking up of that mysterious 'equator-line' between Conscious and Unconscious and the merging of these two worlds into one equally fantastical continent" (507) entails a new model of life in which we recognize that truth is the ongoing reality of phenomenalization itself. There is ultimately nothing 'behind' manifestation. Life is the becoming-manifest of phenomena. Life is essentially the manifestation *of manifestation*. One must reject the Unconscious, "this arbitrarily-invented region, this *other-world*" (506). "Daniel Bush's new theory…abolished this distinction between conscious, and subconscious as arbitrary and dogmatic, and, in place of this hard-and-fast division, regarded the whole ocean of human experience, with all its maddest and most unspeakable delusions, as *always open*" to discovery (506). Accordingly, affectivity is not primarily a surface, not primarily a screen receiving and 'translating' news from the sunken 'other-world' where more powerful things are presumed to be going on. The analyst-phenomenologist does not need to 'interpret' phenomena. What is needed is not interpretation but recognition – not an interpreter who can tell us what things 'really are' but a visionary being who can see *all that there is there to see*. "[N]ot only from the surface of that sea within us *but from all levels and depths of it* we have the power of coming into contact with one another" (506). Ultimately this means that an 'expert' like Bush is no more intelligent as a life-reviewer or mind-reviewer than Sylvanus Cobbold or Gipsy May. Phenomenalization is life, life is affectivity, and affectivity is always absolutely open to itself. In old-style psychoanalysis, the region of affectivity was otherworldly, the analyst being a sort of highpriest who 'communicated' with the transcendent realm. "This region was out of reach, and possessed locked, adamantine gates, as far as our ordinary processes of mental introspection went" (505). If the region of truth, in other words affectivity, is immanent rather than transcendent, there is no need for the one who seeks enlightenment *to transcend*. There is in the final analysis no barrier to cross in the first place. Affectivity is never out of reach. *Nothing* in affectivity is ever out of reach.

The most frightening thing about the inmates who have been imprisoned by traditional psychology-thinking is that they "feel no longer the urge of amorous desire" (511). On a simple level, this merely means that a madhouse is devoid of sex. But as we have seen, 'amorous life' has a wider significance in *Weymouth Sands* – being ultimately nothing less than life itself, in other words affectivity. What is frightening about a madhouse, then, is that it is devoid of *life*. Now the fates of the principal characters differ with respect to the good or bad fortunes of their love-lives; Magnus ends up *without* Curly, whereas Perdita discovers that destiny is on her side. "The Powers have kept us alive. I am on my way to him [Jobber Skald]" (562). But although Magnus feels like one whose heart has become a stone – "Down to the bottom of the world! I'll smile...and smile...and smile – and be a pebble!" (560) – it is impossible to say of him what can be said of the inmates of Hell's Museum ...that existence is devoid of 'amorous life.' For the 'amorous life,' we have already seen, is life itself, is 'Weymouth.' And it is very difficult *not* to imagine Magnus Muir going on living in or as 'Weymouth.'

Magnus can "be a pebble" (560) for the simple reason that in 'Weymouth' *stone* is 'amorous life,' is affectivity. *Stone* may be the fragmented material that makes up 'wet sand' and 'dry sand'; *stone* may be the large object to be used by the Jobber to kill Cattistock; *stone* may be landscape and horizon, as in the intermittent evocations of Portland Bill; *stone* may be the fossil that drops "with a thud" into the bottom of Magnus's coffin now that Curly's deceit phenomenalizes affection as "a solid level of stone, deep in his heart" (545-546); *stone* may be the loved one as Absolute and as universal; "'Whenever you hold in your hand,'" Sylvanus tells Marret, "'a wet pebble by the sea's edge, you must believe you are holding me. Whenever you snatch up a handful of wet sand, by the sea's edge, you must believe I am holding you'" (517). In all these cases, as well as in innumerable others, *stone* is indistinguishable from affectivity. But it is indistinguishable, also, not only from 'amorous life' but from its deliciousness, its very sweetness. In one of the work's most beautiful sections, the love-ruined tutor of classical languages comes to a pool in which he perceives purple and amber-coloured sea-anemones (551). "[T]iny, greenish fish with sharply extended dorsal fins darted to and fro across the waving petals of those plants that were more than plants" (552). Magnus takes notice of "little pyramidal shells with alternate mother-of-pearl bands" (552). He observes "one involved mother-of-pearl shell, with a tiny seaweed actually growing from its surface, the faint roots of which, against the pearl, took on, in those wavering, shifting, broken lights, an indescribable greenish tinge" (552). All of a sudden the mood changes as Magnus comes to think of "the shell-like radiance of his lost girl's flesh." The image "shot through his senses like an arrow, an arrow of sea-pearl!" (552). The "terrible mother-of-pearl arrow" (552) is "terrible" – but it is also "mother-of-pearl"; it still belongs, in other words, to the 'amorous life,' to life as an affective spectacle in which even the death-blow to love is *materially illuminated* by love's "shell-like radiance." Although, for Magnus, love is "the turning into stone of a woman-shell," the "numbness" (546) caused by this petrification does not deprive him of affectivity – for 'numbness' too is affective. 'Numbness' is absolutely affective – which is why numb, stony, insensitive mother-of-pearl is on a par, as radiant absolute, with a forlorn individual whose being trembles in the very last page of the book that tells his story (567).

The arrow of sea-pearl is cruel (552); but it is shot in a world which for some reason has been penetrated by something utterly strange and inexplicable – the "idea of *not* being cruel" (525). This 'idea' is not a unit of cognition in someone's brain but a certitude washing over life as a mystery. It is felt, not in moments of intellectual self-consciousness, but in moments such as those when Magnus Muir becomes vaguely aware of the pleasure he takes in washing his hands with Windsor Soap – "for he loved its healthy, disinfectant smell" (492). "[T]he feeling of washing his hands" involves, precisely *as* feeling, "some new conclusion about life, in its ebbings and flowings, that he had never formulated before, and even now he couldn't quite catch it" (493). The "conclusion" is something Magnus "touched in his mind" (493). *Touching*, here, is not a self-directing. As in the case of 'using' Windsor Soap, of enjoying its smell, there is beforehand a fluid washing-away of any tangible interval between perceiver and perceived. The "conclusion" is an immanency of the mind to itself, just as touching, in the act of washing, is an immanency-to-itself of moving hands, of hands moving through water to produce "an abounding lather" (492). Social, ethical, and metaphysical considerations – hovering in the image of Pilate (492-493) – give way to something closer at hand, immanent at hand, *absolutely* immanent at hand. The sweetness of the smell of Windsor Soap, like the sweetness of "Miss Le Fleau's own piece of private lavender-scented soap lying, pure and sacred, on its own separate china dish" (492), is indistinguishable from the full-brimmed tide, from the inside of Kimmeridge House with the back window looking out on the Spire – in short from affectivity in general and as such. But the sweetness *is* distinguishable from "Italy," from the *transcendent* locus of *transcendent* amorous life understood as a *transcendent* event in and of "the world" (545). In so far as "Italy" (a pleasant place for elopement) is transcendent to 'Weymouth,' it is transcendent *to affectivity*, indeed to 'amorous life' as something other than a trivial pleasure-ground for women who, apart from wanting money, "want to see the world" (545).

In so far as the 'Absolute' is itself conceived as something belonging to the world, it too is transcendent, remote. Accordingly, much like the sweetness of Windsor Soap for Magnus, the sweetness of Marret is for Sylvanus a sweetness that he "can't mix with God" (503). Marret is in a special sense sweeter than God. 'God' here is a *transcendent* 'Absolute,' an 'Absolute' imagined in the way that the world is imagined – imagined, that is, as being extended in the rational space of Euclidian geometry. This *geometric Absolute*, "whose Centre was everywhere and his Circumference nowhere," is a "rounded completeness," in other words a quasi-mathematical totality – one in which, fortunately, there is a fragment "chipped off, leaving a tiny gap" (503). Auto-affectivity, the leading motif of this study, is no such geometric entity but rather an "Absolute [that] had the power of renewing itself from its own ashes" (532). It is this other sense of 'Absolute,' with the concomitant sense of impossible-magical renewal, that is entrusted to those who have been appointed by 'amorous life' for the task of its safekeeping. Perdita and the Jobber are not lovers sharing "mere spiritual affinity" or "mere sexual passion" (565). They are "not just human lovers, not just sweethearts." They are "beyond astonishment, surprise, thankfulness, happiness even" (565). This is so because, rather than simply 'having feelings,' they are indistinguishable from affectivity in general and as such, from feeling as something which, like the 'Absolute,' is at once manifestation and the condition of possibility for manifestation, at once feeling and the condition of possibility for feeling. "[T]hey were animals, old, weak, long-hunted animals, whose love was literally the love of bone for bone, skeleton for skeleton ...Skeletons, literally, they both were!" (565).

Stone is to affectivity what the lover's 'skeleton' is to the lover. Handing Magnus Muir the stone which has been so long in Adam Skald's pocket, Perdita finally remarks that "It's for my old friend, Mr. Gaul. It will keep the Philosophy of Representation from blowing away!" (567). These last words of *Weymouth Sands* are fittingly light-hearted, lifting away all possible sense of the overtragic and oversentimental. But the words perhaps also contain an element of seriousness, in so far as stone is throughout the work suggestive of affectivity, and in so far as any metaphysical thinking directing itself toward life or toward the work may need to foreground affective reality if truth is not to blow away.

BIBLIOGRAPHY

Primary Works

John Cowper Powys

Owen Glendower. London: Picador, 1978 (1941).
Weymouth Sands. London: Picador, 1980 (1935).

Secondary Works

Henry, Michel. *L'Essence de la manifestation*, 2nd edition. Paris: Presses Universitaires de France, 1990 (1963).
—. *The Essence of Manifestation*. Translated by Girard Etzkorn. The Hague: Martinus Nijhoff, 1973.
—. *Généalogie de la psychanalyse: Le commencement perdu*. Paris: Presses Universitaires de France, 1985.
—. *The Genealogy of Psychoanalysis*. Translated by Douglas Brick. Stanford: Stanford University Press, 1993.
—. *Phénoménologie Matérielle*. Paris: Presses Universitaires de France, 1990.

J.R.R. Tolkien
The Books, The Films, The Whole Cultural Phenomenon

by Jeremy Mark Robinson

A new critical study of J.R.R. Tolkien, creator of Middle-earth and author of *The Lord of the Rings*, *The Hobbit* and *The Silmarillion*, among other books.
This new critical study explores Tolkien's major writings (*The Lord of the Rings, The Hobbit, Beowulf: The Monster and the Critics, The Letters, The Silmarillion* and *The History of Middle-earth* volumes); Tolkien and fairy tales; the mythological, political and religious aspects of Tolkien's Middle-earth; the critics' response to Tolkien's fiction over the decades; the Tolkien industry (merchandizing, toys, role-playing games, posters, Tolkien societies, conferences and the like); Tolkien in visual and fantasy art; the cultural aspects of The Lord of the Rings (from the 1950s to the present); Tolkien's fiction's relationship with other fantasy fiction, such as C.S. Lewis and *Harry Potter*; and the TV, radio and film versions of Tolkien's books, including the 2001-03 Hollywood interpretations of *The Lord of the Rings*.
This new book draws on contemporary cultural theory and analysis and offers a sympathetic and illuminating (and sceptical) account of the Tolkien phenomenon. This book is designed to appeal to the general reader (and viewer) of Tolkien: it is written in a clear, jargon-free and easily-accessible style.

754pp   ISBN 1-86171-057-7   £25.00 / $37.50

THE SACRED CINEMA OF ANDREI TARKOVSKY

by Jeremy Mark Robinson

A new study of the Russian filmmaker Andrei Tarkovsky (1932-1986), director of seven feature films, including *Andrei Roublyov, Mirror, Solaris, Stalker* and *The Sacrifice*.
This is one of the most comprehensive and detailed studies of Tarkovsky's cinema available. Every film is explored in depth, with scene-by-scene analyses. All aspects of Tarkovsky's output are critiqued, including editing, camera, staging, script, budget, collaborations, production, sound, music, performance and spirituality. Tarkovsky is placed with a European New Wave tradition of filmmaking, alongside directors like Ingmar Bergman, Carl Theodor Dreyer, Pier Paolo Pasolini and Robert Bresson.
An essential addition to film studies.

Illustrations: 150 b/w, 4 colour. 682 pages. First edition. Hardback.

Publisher: Crescent Moon Publishing. Distributor: Gardners Books.

ISBN 1-86171-096-8 (9781861710963) £60.00 / $105.00

The Best of Peter Redgrove's Poetry
The Book of Wonders

by Peter Redgrove, edited and introduced by Jeremy Robinson

Poems of wet shirts and 'wonder-awakening dresses'; honey, wasps and bees; orchards and apples; rivers, seas and tides; storms, rain, weather and clouds; waterworks; labyrinths; amazing perfumes; the Cornish landscape (Penzance, Perranporth, Falmouth, Boscastle, the Lizard and Scilly Isles); the sixth sense and 'extra-sensuous perception'; witchcraft; alchemical vessels and laboratories; yoga; menstruation; mines, minerals and stones; sand dunes; mud-baths; mythology; dreaming; vulvas; and lots of sex magic. This book gathers together poetry (and prose) from every stage of Redgrove's career, and every book. It includes pieces that have only appeared in small presses and magazines, and in uncollected form.

'Peter Redgrove is really an extraordinary poet' (George Szirtes, *Quarto* magazine)
'Peter Redgrove is one of the few significant poets now writing... His 'means' are indeed brilliant and delightful. Technically he is a poet essentially of brilliant and unexpected images...he never disappoints' (Kathleen Raine, *Temenos* magazine).

240pp   ISBN 1-86171-063-1   2nd edition   £19.99 / $29.50

Sex–Magic–Poetry–Cornwall
A Flood of Poems

by Peter Redgrove. Edited with an essay by Jeremy Robinson

A marvellous collection of poems by one of Britain's best but underrated poets, Peter Redgrove. This book brings together some of Redgrove's wildest and most passionate works, creating a 'flood' of poetry. Philip Hobsbaum called Redgrove 'the great poet of our time', while Angela Carter said: 'Redgrove's language can light up a page.' Redgrove ranks alongside Ted Hughes and Sylvia Plath. He is in every way a 'major poet'. Robinson's essay analyzes all of Redgrove's poetic work, including his use of sex magic, natural science, menstruation, psychology, myth, alchemy and feminism.
A new edition, including a new introduction, new preface and new bibliography.

'Robinson's enthusiasm is winning, and his perceptive readings are supported by a very useful bibliography' (*Acumen* magazine)
'*Sex-Magic-Poetry-Cornwall* is a very rich essay... It is like a brightly-lighted box. (Peter Redgrove)
'This is an excellent selection of poetry and an extensive essay on the themes and theories of this unusual poet by Jeremy Robinson' (*Chapman* magazine)

220pp   New, 3rd edition   ISBN 1-86171-070-4   £14.99 / $23.50

THE ART OF ANDY GOLDSWORTHY

COMPLETE WORKS: SPECIAL EDITION
(PAPERBACK and HARDBACK)

by William Malpas

A new, special edition of the study of the contemporary British sculptor, Andy Goldsworthy, including a new introduction, new bibliography and many new illustrations.

This is the most comprehensive, up-to-date, well-researched and in-depth account of Goldsworthy's art available anywhere.

Andy Goldsworthy makes land art. His sculpture is a sensitive, intuitive response to nature, light, time, growth, the seasons and the earth. Goldsworthy's environmental art is becoming ever more popular: 1993's art book *Stone* was a bestseller; the press raved about Goldsworthy taking over a number of London West End art galleries in 1994; during 1995 Goldsworthy designed a set of Royal Mail stamps and had a show at the British Museum. Malpas surveys all of Goldsworthy's art, and analyzes his relation with other land artists such as Robert Smithson, Walter de Maria, Richard Long and David Nash, and his place in the contemporary British art scene.

The Art of Andy Goldsworthy discusses all of Goldsworthy's important and recent exhibitions and books, including the *Sheepfolds* project; the TV documentaries; *Wood* (1996); the New York Holocaust memorial (2003); and Goldsworthy's collaboration on a dance performance.

Illustrations: 70 b/w, 1 colour. 330 pages. New, special, 2nd edition.
Publisher: Crescent Moon Publishing. Distributor: Gardners Books.

ISBN 1-86171-059-3 (9781861710598) (Paperback) £25.00 / $44.00

ISBN 1-86171-080-1 (9781861710802) (Hardback) £60.00 / $105.00

CRESCENT MOON PUBLISHING

ARTS, PAINTING, SCULPTURE

The Art of Andy Goldsworthy: Complete Works(Pbk)
The Art of Andy Goldsworthy: Complete Works (Hbk)
Andy Goldsworthy in Close-Up (Pbk)
Andy Goldsworthy in Close-Up (Hbk)
Land Art: A Complete Guide
Richard Long: The Art of Walking
The Art of Richard Long: Complete Works (Pbk)
The Art of Richard Long: Complete Works (Hbk)
Richard Long in Close-Up
Land Art In the UK
Land Art in Close-Up
Installation Art in Close-Up
Minimal Art and Artists In the 1960s and After
Colourfield Painting
Land Art DVD, TV documentary
Andy Goldsworthy DVD, TV documentary

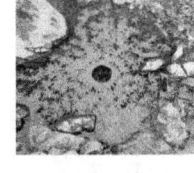

The Erotic Object: Sexuality in Sculpture From Prehistory to the Present Day
Sex in Art: Pornography and Pleasure in Painting and Sculpture
Postwar Art
Sacred Gardens: The Garden in Myth, Religion and Art
Glorification: Religious Abstraction in Renaissance and 20th Century Art
Early Netherlandish Painting
Leonardo da Vinci
Piero della Francesca
Giovanni Bellini
Fra Angelico: Art and Religion in the Renaissance
Mark Rothko: The Art of Transcendence
Frank Stella: American Abstract Artist
Jasper Johns: Painting By Numbers
Brice Marden
Alison Wilding: The Embrace of Sculpture
Vincent van Gogh: Visionary Landscapes
Eric Gill: Nuptials of God
Constantin Brancusi: Sculpting the Essence of Things
Max Beckmann
Egon Schiele: Sex and Death In Purple Stockings
Delizioso Fotografico Fervore: Works In Process 1
Sacro Cuore: Works In Process 2
The Light Eternal: J.M.W. Turner
The Madonna Glorified: Karen Arthurs

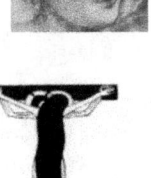

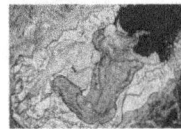

LITERATURE

J.R.R. Tolkien: The Books, The Films, The Whole Cultural Phenomenon
Harry Potter
Sexing Hardy: Thomas Hardy and Feminism
Thomas Hardy's *Tess of the d'Urbervilles*
Thomas Hardy's *Jude the Obscure*
Thomas Hardy: The Tragic Novels
Love and Tragedy: Thomas Hardy
The Poetry of Landscape in Hardy
Wessex Revisited: Thomas Hardy and John Cowper Powys
Wolfgang Iser: Essays
Petrarch, Dante and the Troubadours
Maurice Sendak and the Art of Children's Book Illustration
Andrea Dworkin
Cixous, Irigaray, Kristeva: The *Jouissance* of French Feminism
Julia Kristeva: Art, Love, Melancholy, Philosophy, Semiotics and Psychoanalysis
Hélène Cixous I Love You: The *Jouissance* of Writing
Luce Irigaray: Lips, Kissing, and the Politics of Sexual Difference
Peter Redgrove: Here Comes the Flood
Peter Redgrove: Sex-Magic-Poetry-Cornwall
Lawrence Durrell: Between Love and Death, East and West
Love, Culture & Poetry: Lawrence Durrell
Cavafy: Anatomy of a Soul
German Romantic Poetry: Goethe, Novalis, Heine, Hölderlin, Schlegel, Schiller
Feminism and Shakespeare
Shakespeare: Selected Sonnets
Shakespeare: Love, Poetry & Magic
The Passion of D.H. Lawrence
D.H. Lawrence: Symbolic Landscapes
D.H. Lawrence: Infinite Sensual Violence
Rimbaud: Arthur Rimbaud and the Magic of Poetry
The Ecstasies of John Cowper Powys
Sensualism and Mythology: The Wessex Novels of John Cowper Powys
Amorous Life: John Cowper Powys and the Manifestation of Affectivity (H.W. Fawkner)
Postmodern Powys: New Essays on John Cowper Powys (Joe Boulter)
Rethinking Powys: Critical Essays on John Cowper Powys
Paul Bowles & Bernardo Bertolucci
Rainer Maria Rilke
In the Dim Void: Samuel Beckett
Samuel Beckett Goes into the Silence
André Gide: Fiction and Fervour
Jackie Collins and the Blockbuster Novel
Blinded By Her Light: The Love-Poetry of Robert Graves
The Passion of Colours: Travels In Mediterranean Lands
Poetic Forms
The Dolphin-Boy

POETRY

The Best of Peter Redgrove's Poetry
Peter Redgrove: Here Comes The Flood
Peter Redgrove: Sex-Magic-Poetry-Cornwall
Ursula Le Guin: Walking In Cornwall
Dante: Selections From the Vita Nuova
Petrarch, Dante and the Troubadours
William Shakespeare: Selected Sonnets
Blinded By Her Light: The Love-Poetry of Robert Graves
Emily Dickinson: Selected Poems
Emily Brontë: Poems
Thomas Hardy: Selected Poems
Percy Bysshe Shelley: Poems
John Keats: Selected Poems
D.H. Lawrence: Selected Poems
Edmund Spenser: Poems
John Donne: Poems
Henry Vaughan: Poems
Sir Thomas Wyatt: Poems
Robert Herrick: Selected Poems
Rilke: Space, Essence and Angels in the Poetry of Rainer Maria Rilke
Rainer Maria Rilke: Selected Poems
Friedrich Hölderlin: Selected Poems
Arseny Tarkovsky: Selected Poems
Arthur Rimbaud: Selected Poems
Arthur Rimbaud: A Season in Hell
Arthur Rimbaud and the Magic of Poetry
D.J. Enright: By-Blows
Jeremy Reed: Brigitte's Blue Heart
Jeremy Reed: Claudia Schiffer's Red Shoes
Gorgeous Little Orpheus
Radiance: New Poems
Crescent Moon Book of Nature Poetry
Crescent Moon Book of Love Poetry
Crescent Moon Book of Mystical Poetry
Crescent Moon Book of Elizabethan Love Poetry
Crescent Moon Book of Metaphysical Poetry
Crescent Moon Book of Romantic Poetry
Pagan America: New American Poetry

MEDIA, CINEMA, FEMINISM and CULTURAL STUDIES

J.R.R. Tolkien: The Books, The Films, The Whole Cultural Phenomenon
Harry Potter
Cixous, Irigaray, Kristeva: The *Jouissance* of French Feminism
Julia Kristeva: Art, Love, Melancholy, Philosophy, Semiotics and Psychoanalysis
Luce Irigaray: Lips, Kissing, and the Politics of Sexual Difference
Hélène Cixous I Love You: The *Jouissance* of Writing
Andrea Dworkin
'Cosmo Woman': The World of Women's Magazines
Women in Pop Music
Discovering the Goddess (Geoffrey Ashe)
The Poetry of Cinema
The Sacred Cinema of Andrei Tarkovsky (Pbk and Hbk)
Paul Bowles & Bernardo Bertolucci
Media Hell: Radio, TV and the Press
An Open Letter to the BBC
Detonation Britain: Nuclear War in the UK
Feminism and Shakespeare
Wild Zones: Pornography, Art and Feminism
Sex in Art: Pornography and Pleasure in Painting and Sculpture
Sexing Hardy: Thomas Hardy and Feminism

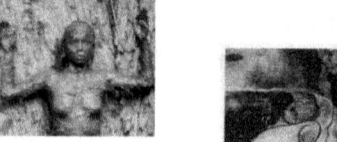
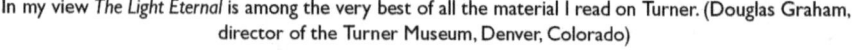

In my view *The Light Eternal* is among the very best of all the material I read on Turner. (Douglas Graham, director of the Turner Museum, Denver, Colorado)

The Light Eternal is a model monograph, an exemplary job. The subject matter of the book is beautifully organised and dead on beam. (Lawrence Durrell)

It is amazing for me to see my work treated with such passion and respect. (Andrea Dworkin)

Sex-Magic-Poetry-Cornwall is a very rich essay... It is like a brightly-lighted box. (Peter Redgrove)

CRESCENT MOON PUBLISHING
P.O. Box 393, Maidstone, Kent, ME14 5XU, United Kingdom.
01622-729593 (UK) 01144-1622-729593 (US) 0044-1622-729593 (other territories)
cresmopub@yahoo.co.uk   www.crescentmoon.org.uk

www.ingramcontent.com/pod-product-compliance
Lightning Source LLC
LaVergne TN
LVHW022341080426
835508LV00012BA/1299